this book is dedicated to

~~~~~~~~~~~~

my beautiful boys Fox & Malakai.
never stop getting messy, chasing
creativity & seeing the world
through adventurous eyes.

TABLE OF CONTENTS

ABOUT SUNEE SIDE UP

I know what you're thinking, *"not another cookbook"*... but hear me out!

This beautiful book is jam-packed with healthy recipes that will satisfy your cravings, nourish your body, and leave everyone questioning, "how the heck was that 'Caramelised Goddess Pizza' healthy, and where do I get me some more?!" (psst... it's on page 137).

This is a cookbook full of old-school cooking and recipes with a modern-day and healthy twist. Think – your mum's cooking blended with a Byron Bay healthy café (does that make sense to anyone else but me!?)

Whether you're making a wholesome pasta for the family on a Tuesday night, lamington bites with your kids on a Saturday morning or impressing your mates with my Luxe Vegan Cannelloni, there are recipes for everyone and every occasion!

My vision for this book is for you to make it **MESSY!** I want to see flour fingerprints on the cover, honey stains on the spine and crumbs of almond meal scattered in the pages. Enjoy it, embrace it and pass it down.

All recipes in this book have been approved by a registered Dietitian and Nutritionist (see our healthy queens below). I've also made it simple and quick to identify which recipes cater to your or your family's dietary requirements. Check the bottom right corner of each recipe to determine if it suits your eating style! These dietary requirements include:

GF	Gluten Free	**LOW FODMAP**	
DF	Dairy Free	Modern **Paleo**	
NF	Nut Free	**V**	Vegan
		VG	Vegetarian

I hope these recipes **INSPIRE** you to embrace and enjoy healthy cooking and mix up your go-to household recipes. It's time to create memories around the kitchen bench with the kids and at the dining table with the whole family.

I hope you love this book as much as I've enjoyed creating it.

♡ Sarah

DEE ZIBARA
Nutritionist

MILLIE PADULA
Dietician

HELPFUL NOTES

 Be sure to check the label and ensure the ingredients match your dietary requirements.

 Oats: Gluten free oats are not suitable for those with coeliac disease. To ensure your recipe is completely gluten free, please replace oats with quinoa flakes.

 This recipe contains alcohol, but can be removed/replaced with non-alcoholic options.

PANTRY STAPLES

vegan choc chips

organic herbs/ spices

nutritional yeast

chia seeds

chickpeas/beans

oats

coconut oil

tahini

Plant-based milk

herbal tea

organic cacao

blanched almond meal

honey

quinoa

organic bone broth

pure maple syrup

arrowroot/tapioca starch

3

buckwheat/
gluten free
flour

extra virgin
olive oil

buckwheat/gluten free pasta

desiccated
coconut

dried chilli
flakes

large free
range eggs

vanilla bean
paste

coconut
flakes

gluten free
baking powder

fresh herbs

coconut
sugar

mixed nuts

high quality
salt

coconut aminos/
tamari sauce

frozen berries

fresh Medjool
dates

buckwheat
groats/kernels

firm tofu

canned
coconut cream

vegan protein
powder

apple cider
vinegar

KITCHEN STAPLES

whisk

cast-iron pot

food processor

mortar and pestle

measuring cups

ceramic baking dish

wooden spoon

| STOP | AUTO | PULSE |

garlic crusher

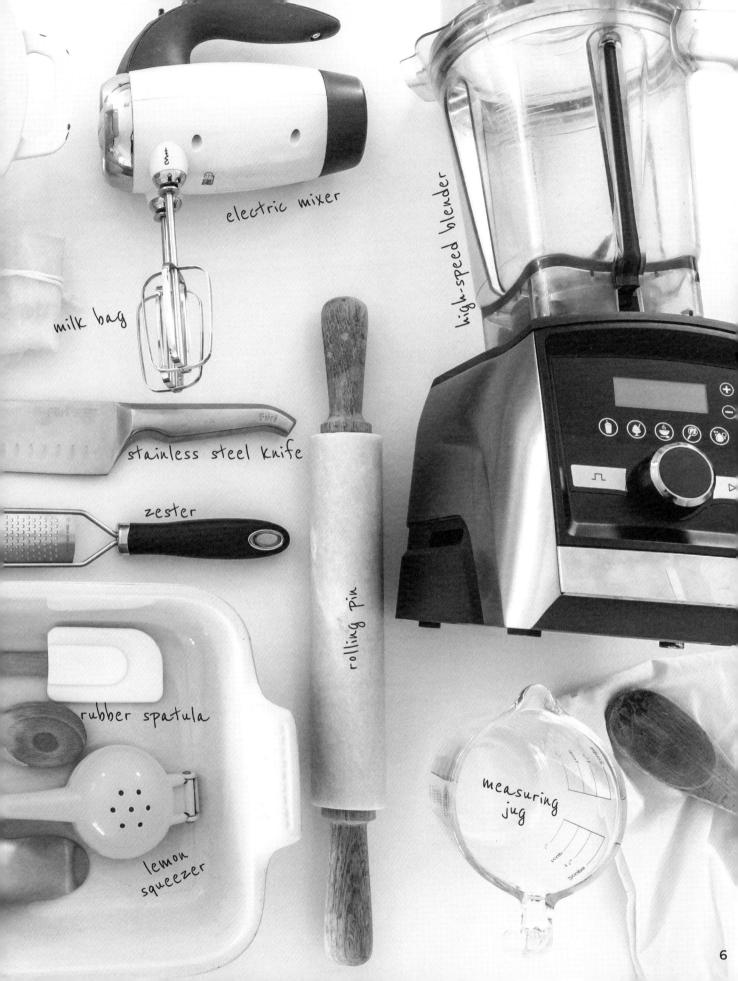

electric mixer

high-speed blender

milk bag

stainless steel knife

zester

rolling pin

rubber spatula

lemon squeezer

measuring jug

6

COOKING BASICS
Vegetables

1. Preheat the oven to 180°C (355°F) and line a baking tray with baking paper

2. Wash the sweet potato before peeling as there may be a lot of dirt

3. Peel the skin off the sweet potato using a peeler, or leave the skin on for a more rustic look (just ensure it is washed well)

4. For the pumpkin, you can try to use a peeler but if it is too hard (yes we think this is too hard), cut the pumpkin into quarters so you have a flat surface to lay the pumpkin on and carefully trim the skin using a sharp knife

5. Cut the sweet potato/pumpkin into large cubes and place in a bowl. Drizzle olive oil and seasonings (if desired) on top and toss with your hands or tongs to coat evenly

6. Place on your prepared baking tray and bake in the oven for 35–45 minutes. You can turn pieces around halfway through cooking to ensure they roast evenly by using a spatula or a pair of tongs

7. To test to see if a piece is done, carefully pull the tray out and using a fork or sharp knife, insert it into the vegetable. If it goes in and out with ease, you know it's ready!

8. Pumpkin does cook quicker than sweet potato, so you may want to use 2 trays or keep the pumpkin on one side of the tray to make it easier to remove from the oven first

9. Remove from the oven and season with pink salt to taste

Tip: We like to use the small white and red potatoes with fresh rosemary for roasting!

1. Preheat the oven to 180°C (355°F)

2. Wash potatoes, cut in half and place in a large ceramic baking dish or baking tray

3. Drizzle a generous amount of good quality oil over potatoes (we often use extra virgin olive oil or avocado oil), a sprinkle of salt and fresh rosemary roughly chopped. Toss or mix well using your hands, ensuring all potatoes are evenly coated with oil

4. Roast in the oven for 40 minutes or until potatoes are golden brown. You can turn potatoes halfway through cooking using a spatula or a pair of tongs to ensure they roast evenly and don't stick to the bottom of the tray/dish

5. Remove and add pink salt to taste (if you need more)

Zucchini Noodles (Zoodles)

1. Use a spiralizer and follow appliance instructions to create easy zoodles

2. If you don't own a spiralizer you can DIY zoodles using a julienne peeler, mandoline or if you're up for the challenge, a sharp knife and a lot of patience (we don't have the patience for this), to slice zucchini into long, thin noodle-like strips

1. Wash thoroughly ensuring to coat each curl of the leaf with water

2. Using a knife, cut along the edge of the stalk or tear the leaves away with your hands to separate from the stalk

3. When using raw kale for a salad it can be quite bitter and tough. To make it more tender and easier to digest, place torn kale in a bowl with a small amount of olive oil and lemon juice and massage with your hands for 3–5 minutes

CAULIFLOWER RICE

1. Cut cauliflower into florets and using a food processor, pulse the florets in small batches until you've reached a similar consistency to rice

2. Again, taking small batches of the cauli rice, place into a linen tea towel (or a nut milk bag), fold the tea towel over and take the cauliflower bundle in one hand and with the other, hold the empty tea towel and twist. This will squeeze out any excess liquid

3. Enjoy cauli rice raw in a nourish bowl or cook for a warm meal. We usually add it to a wok in a stir-fry or heat in a large cast-iron pot/saucepan with a dash of sesame oil, salt and spices

QUINOA

Ratio: 1 cup of dry quinoa to 2 cups of water

1. In a strainer, rinse quinoa under cold running water. This removes the natural coating called saponin which will help to remove the bitter taste

2. In a small saucepan over a high heat, add 2 cups of water and the rinsed quinoa. Bring to a boil

3. Allow quinoa to boil for 1–2 minutes then remove from heat

4. Cover with a lid and set aside for 15 minutes. This will allow the quinoa to absorb the water without turning to mush

5. Using your strainer again, carefully pour quinoa into a strainer to drain excess water

6. Fluff quinoa with a fork before serving

ZESTING

1. Using a microplane is super easy and requires minimal effort. It's very versatile and you can use it for grating fresh ginger and garlic, whole nutmeg or even fresh coconut! When zesting citrus, remove only the top layer of the skin of the fruit. If you zest the pith (the white stuff) it will be bitter

CHILLI PREP

Chef Tip: When dealing with a very hot chilli, we advise wearing gloves.

1. To deseed a chilli use a small sharp knife and slice the chilli in half lengthways. Keeping the chilli cut-side up on the chopping board, use the back of a small knife or a teaspoon to remove the seeds and the white membrane

2. Finely chop your chilli or prepare as the recipe instructs

Melted Vegan Chocolate

1. Pour water in a small saucepan until it's around 3–4cm (1–1.5in) deep. Bring to a boil and reduce to a simmer

2. Place a heatproof bowl in the rim of the saucepan so it's sitting comfortably but not touching the boiling water (this is extremely important, otherwise your chocolate will burn)

3. Place chocolate shards, squares or buttons in the bowl and stir until smooth and almost completely melted

4. We like to take it off the heat just before all lumps are gone to ensure we never burn the chocolate. Continue to stir in the warm bowl until completely melted

COOKING BASICS
Chicken

1. Fill a saucepan with water and bring to a gentle simmer (we like to add a little pink Himalayan salt to our water for enhanced flavour)

2. Place chicken breast in the water

3. Allow 15–20 minutes of cooking time per 500g (1.1lb) of chicken

4. To check if it's cooked through, remove from the saucepan and cut a small section in the thickest part. The juices should run clear and the flesh will be white in colour

5. Once cooked through remove and allow to cool

We usually prepare around 2–3 chicken breasts each time we make shredded chicken for meal preps. Slow cooked chicken breast is super simple and efficient!

1. Place 2–3 chicken breasts in the slow cooker (cannot be frozen) along with a few generous pinches of pink salt, pepper and fresh herbs (we like a few sprigs of rosemary). Then cover with enough room temp water (or stock for more flavour) so the breasts are fully submerged

2. Set your slow cooker to low and allow chicken to cook for a little over 3 hours (this will vary depending on your slow cooker). Alternatively, if you have a probe, test chicken and remove from the slow cooker when the internal temperature has reached around 75°C (165°F)

3. Remove chicken from the slow cooker and shred! Our fave, simple shredding technique is in a food processor. Blitz chicken for a few seconds or use two forks to shred chicken manually

Based on a 1.4kg (3lb) chicken

1. Preheat oven to 200°C (390°F) fan forced

2. Line a baking tray with baking paper or lightly grease a roasting pan with oil

3. Rinse chicken, washing inside and out under cold water. Pat dry with paper towel (ensure to dry thoroughly and remove all moisture or else the skin won't turn crispy)

4. Stuff the inside of the chicken with flavours of your choice. Our favourite is a few sprigs of fresh rosemary, 2 cloves of garlic and a lemon cut into quarters (microwave the lemon until hot before stuffing inside the chicken – this helps it cook evenly)

5. Drizzle the outside of the chicken with olive oil and cover evenly using a pastry brush or your hands. Season generously with pink salt, pepper and mixed herbs (optional). We also like to tie the legs together with kitchen string to keep the stuffing flavour inside, as well as making it easier to manoeuvre the chicken

6. Place chicken (breast-side down) onto tray/pan

7. Roast for 20 minutes. Turn chicken over, breast-side up and continue to roast for a further 40 minutes, basting during cooking

8. To check if the chicken is cooked, take a small sharp knife and pierce the thickest part of the thigh. The juices should run clear. If it's a little pink, return to the oven for 5–10 minutes and then test again

Red Meat

There are many different cuts of steak and this makes a big difference to the cooking time, taste and texture, so be sure to select the right one for your recipe

1. Choose a pan that has a lot of room for the steak to move. Avoid overcrowding or squishing a lot of steaks into one pan

2. You can turn the steak every minute of the recommended cooking time for the best caramelised crust

3. Salt your steak in advance! Allow 2 hours for every 1cm (0.5in) of thickness to give the steak time to absorb the salt and become seasoned throughout

1. Sprinkle a generous amount of cracked pepper and pink salt onto a plate and press your steak into it moments before you place it in the pan

2. Preheat a fry pan on high until hot but not smoking

3. Drizzle a small amount of oil into the pan and leave for a moment

4. Add the steak and sear evenly on each side for our recommended time (see steak timings right)

5. Take your steak out of the pan and cover with some foil. Let it rest for double the amount of time you cooked it for. This will help the juices settle and reabsorb into the meat so they don't all run out when you cut it

(Timings based on a 2.2cm (1in) thick steak)

Well Done

Cook for approximately 4-6 minutes on each side.

Sear on one side until moisture pools on top of the steak then flip until the same thing happens on the other side. It will have a slight pink colour and will feel resistant when tongs are pressed against it.

Chef Tip: Press your thumb and pinky finger together and with the other hand, feel the part of your palm just below your thumb. This level of resistance means well done!

Medium

Cook for approximately 3-4 minutes on each side.

Sear on one side until moisture pools on top of the steak then cook on the second side for the same result. It will look pale pink in the middle with hardly any juice. It will feel firm and springy when tongs are pressed on top.

Chef Tip: Press your thumb and ring finger together and with the other hand feel the part of your palm just below your thumb. This level of resistance means medium!

Rare

Sear for a few minutes on either side of steak depending on thickness. Meat will be dark in colour and will feel soft and spongy with a slight resistance when pressed with tongs.

Chef Tip: Press your thumb and index finger together and with the other hand feel the part of your palm just below your thumb. This is rare!

COOKING BASICS
Eggs

FRIED

1. Heat a flat fry pan on low-medium heat. This will help to cook the egg evenly and gently

2. Add your choice of oil to evenly coat the base of the pan

3. Crack egg into the pan. The egg white will change to an opaque colour when it's cooked

4. If you like to flip your eggs, take a spatula and slide it under the egg and with a quick flick of the wrist and keeping the egg close to the pan, flip it so the yolk is now facing down. Take it off now if you like yours over easy!

5. For well done, keep the egg in the pan and check the yolk by lightly touching it with the spatula, it will feel a little bouncy

Chef Tip: Instead of flipping the eggs to cook them more, place a saucepan lid over the eggs as soon as you crack them into the pan. The trapped heat will cook the eggs gently (you're welcome)!

SCRAMBLED

1. Crack your desired number of eggs into a bowl and season with salt and pepper

2. Take a fork and whisk eggs until pale yellow and little bubbles have formed on top of the liquid

3. Heat a flat fry pan on medium heat and add your choice of oil to coat the pan

4. Pour in egg mixture and wait a few seconds until you see the mixture set around the edges

5. Using a spatula, push the egg mixture away from the sides of the pan and repeat the whole way around the pan, letting the uncooked egg run into the free space. This will create ribbons and won't let your eggs become rubbery

6. Repeat this until the eggs are cooked to your liking

POACHED

1. Add water to a deep saucepan until approximately ⅔ full. We find this the easiest way to poach an egg because it has more time to form that perfect teardrop shape!

2. Bring to the boil and add a dash (roughly 2 tsp) of vinegar to the water before reducing to a simmer; you should see bubbles coming up to the surface but not popping

3. Crack an egg into a small bowl

4. Carefully slide the egg into the simmering water

5. Use a timer and cook for 3–3½ minutes for poached eggs with firm whites and soft, runny yolks, or 4–5 minutes for firmer yolk (we remove ours after 3 minutes and 15 seconds . . . yes we're very specific about our runny poached eggs here)

6. Remove eggs from the water with a slotted spoon and serve immediately

Chef Tip: There are many different theories on poaching an egg. If this one doesn't work for you, try stirring the water with a spoon to form a whirlpool before step 4.

Hand Method

1. Crack egg on the edge of a bowl and pour the contents into the palm of your hand, placing it over a bowl of course! Wiggle your fingers and let the egg white slip between them into the bowl

2. You will be left with a clean egg yolk in your palm

Shell Method

1. Crack the egg on the edge of a bowl and gently tip the white and the yolk from one half of the shell to the other, letting the white slip through each time into the bowl and leaving the yolk on one side of the egg shell

Chef Tip: The best way to remove any scrap of unwanted shell is to use a half of the egg shell like a magnetic scoop. Believe us, this is game-changing!

1. Fill a saucepan with cold water and gently lower eggs into the water using a spoon

2. Place the pan over a medium heat and bring to a gentle boil for 3–5 minutes

Cooking Times

- 3 minutes for very soft yolks and barely set whites

- 4 minutes for runny yolks and well set whites

- 5 minutes for firm yolks

- For hard-boiled eggs, boil for 8 minutes and then pour out water from the saucepan and run plenty of cold water over the eggs. This stops the cooking process and also stops the grey ring forming around the yolk

Chef Tip: Allow eggs to come to room temperature before boiling to reduce the risk of cracking when submerged.

Vegetables – Simmer, Boil & Blanch

1. Fill a bowl with water and ice cubes (this is called an ice bath), and have a slotted spoon ready

2. Fill a pot ⅔ with water and bring to the boil

3. Prepare desired vegetables to be blanched

4. Place the vegetables in the boiling water in batches so the water never drops below the boil

5. Set a timer and after 30 seconds, take out one vegetable to test and submerge immediately in the ice bath. Taste to ensure the vegetable is cooked to your liking

6. If the vegetable is not cooked to your liking, place it back into boiling water for a further 30 seconds at a time

7. When they are cooked, take your slotted spoon and scoop them out of the boiling water and place them straight into the ice bath. This immediately stops the cooking process

When liquid boils, large bubbles rise rapidly to the surface and pop.

The key to maintaining a boil is to use plenty of liquid so that when you add food, it does not reduce the heat of the liquid dramatically and slow down the process. You may find it helpful to add food gradually rather than all at once as this will help the liquid to maintain its heat

A simmer is when a small bubble or two breaks the surface of the liquid every second or two. If there are lots of bubbles or the bubbles are large, lower the temperature

13

BREKKIE

OMELETTE TOAST

SERVES 2-4

INGREDIENTS

4 slices gluten free bread

4 eggs

salt & pepper to taste

1 tsp coconut oil

50g (1.8oz) or 2 slices shaved deli chicken (finely diced)

½ small tomato (finely diced)

small handful baby spinach (finely chopped)

Sweet 'n' Creamy Drizzle

1 tbsp hulled tahini

1 tsp apple cider vinegar

2 tsp honey

2 tsp Dijon mustard

1 tbsp almond milk

salt to taste

dried chilli flakes

METHOD

1. Use a sharp knife to cut a generous hole from the centre of each slice of bread

2. Crack eggs into a small bowl and whisk together until fluffy. Add a few generous cracks of salt and pepper then mix well

3. Heat a drizzle of coconut oil in a large fry pan over medium heat. Once coconut oil has melted, place 2 slices of gluten free bread (with the centre removed) onto the pan

4. To ensure you get an even amount of each ingredient on each slice of toast, take ¼ of the sliced chicken and scatter it into the open hole in the centre of the bread. Do the same with the diced tomato and chopped baby spinach. Then pour ¼ of the egg mixture (this is around 3½ tbsp) into the centre of the hole, covering the diced chicken, tomato and baby spinach

5. If you have a lid for your large fry pan, cover and allow it to cook on one side for 2 minutes. If you don't have a lid, that's ok too!

6. Flip each slice of bread over, allowing it to cook on the other side. You want each side of the omelette toast to be slightly golden

7. Add another drizzle of coconut oil to the pan before cooking the other two slices

8. Mix all Sweet 'n' Creamy Drizzle ingredients together in a small bowl to form the dressing

9. Place two slices of omelette toast on two separate plates. Top with drizzle, a crack of salt, pepper and a sprinkle of dried chilli flakes. Serve hot!

DF GF LOW FODMAP

16

EGGS BENNY

INGREDIENTS

see page 11

2 poached eggs

1 gluten free seeded bun

2 slices smoked salmon

Hollandaise Sauce

2 large egg yolks   *see page 12*

1 tbsp lemon juice

salt & pepper

sprinkle sweet paprika

1 small garlic clove

⅓ cup coconut oil (melted)

1 tbsp hulled tahini

2 tbsp hot water   *or as much as needed*

Toppings

1 stem spring onion (finely chopped)

1 tbsp fresh parsley

¼ tsp pink salt

METHOD

1. Add several cups of boiling water to your food processor and allow to sit while you poach the eggs. This is important so your appliance is warm and helps to warm up the sauce

2. Pour boiling water out of your food processor and pat dry. Add egg yolks, lemon juice, salt, pepper, paprika and garlic powder and blitz on low until combined

3. While the food processor is on low speed, slowly add in melted coconut oil and tahini and continue blending until sauce thickens. Add hot water to achieve a thinner consistency

4. Meanwhile, halve a gluten free seeded bun and place both halves in your toaster

5. Assemble your Eggs Benny by placing bun halves onto a plate, top with smoked salmon, poached egg and Hollandaise sauce. Garnish with spring onion, parsley and a little extra pink salt

taste test and add more spice/salt if necessary

DF GF NF

CORN & ZUCCHINI FRITTERS

MAKES 15 FRITTERS

INGREDIENTS

1 can (420g/15oz) corn kernels (drained)

2 cups zucchini (grated)

¼ red onion (diced)

2 sprigs coriander

1 cup buckwheat flour

1 tsp pink salt

½ tsp baking powder

½ tsp paprika

1 egg

1 stem spring onion (thinly sliced)

2 tbsp coconut oil

METHOD

1. Add all ingredients except coconut oil to a large bowl and mix together well

2. Heat coconut oil in a large fry pan on medium-high heat. Once heated, use a tablespoon to scoop out the mixture and place into the pan. We cooked 5 in the pan at once (3 batches)

3. Cook for 1½-2 minutes on each side until golden

4. Remove from the pan and place onto a plate lined with paper towel

5. Repeat until all fritters are cooked. Serve with Fritter Brekkie Bowl or enjoy on their own!

DF GF NF VG

FRITTER BREKKIE BOWL

SERVES 1

INGREDIENTS

8 vine tomatoes

8 button mushrooms (halved)

1 sweet potato (cut in half lengthways then into strips)

1 tsp coconut oil

1 tbsp lemon juice

3 stalks kale (stem removed & roughly chopped)

3 rashers nitrate-free bacon

1 egg (poached) → see page 11

2 Corn & Zucchini Fritters

½ avocado → see page 19

¼ lime

METHOD

1. Preheat oven to 190°C (375°F) and line baking trays with baking paper

2. Place tomatoes and mushrooms on 1 tray and sweet potato on the other tray. Bake the tomatoes and mushrooms for 15 minutes. Bake sweet potato for 30 minutes

3. While your veggies bake, heat coconut oil in a small fry pan over medium heat. Add lemon juice and kale and toss for 30-45 seconds or until vibrant green. Remove from the heat and add to your serving bowl

4. In the same fry pan, cook bacon until crispy (or to your preference)

5. Prepare poached egg and remove vegetables from the oven

6. Assemble the remainder of your bowl and serve with avocado and lime!

DF GF NF

BRUNCH 'N' BOWL ～～～

SERVES 2

INGREDIENTS

or 2 large wedges →

450g (16oz) Kent pumpkin (deseeded & sliced into 2 thick wedges)

1 tbsp olive oil

pink salt

2 large eggs

¼ cup of your fave Sunee dip ⟶

See page 227

10 vine tomatoes (or 2 even vines)

2 thick slices of paleo bread (or bread of your choice)

2 cups kale (washed & stem removed)

½ large avocado

1-2 tbsp black sesame seeds

METHOD

1. Preheat oven to 180°C (355°F) and line a tray with baking paper

2. Place each wedge of pumpkin on the baking tray, brush with a little olive oil, and coat with a generous sprinkle of pink salt. Bake in the oven for 30-40 minutes or until pumpkin is completely soft and cooked through

3. Meanwhile, softly boil 2 large eggs and prepare your chosen dip

4. 15 minutes before your pumpkin finishes baking, coat vine tomatoes in olive oil and a crack of pink salt and place on the same tray as the pumpkin to bake for 10-15 minutes. (You should be able to remove the tray from the oven with the pumpkin wedges completely cooked through and the vine tomatoes roasted to perfection with the skins beginning to peel off)

see page 11

be careful when placing tomatoes in the tray as it will be scorching hot

5. While you wait for the tomatoes to bake in the oven, toast your bread and roughly chop kale leaves. Coat kale with a little olive oil and pink salt then place in a small fry pan and cook over medium heat until wilted

6. Cut your ½ avocado in ½ again and roll in black sesame seeds

7. Prepare two serving bowls with equal portions of each ingredient to create the ultimate brunch 'n' bowl

DF GF NF VG

VANILLA PROTEIN GRANOLA

MAKES 4 CUPS OR 1 LARGE JAR

INGREDIENTS

1 cup gluten free oats (or quinoa flakes)

1 cup coconut chips/large flakes

⅓ cup sultanas (or dried fruit of choice)

½ cup cashews (roughly chopped)

½ cup dry roasted almonds
(roughly chopped)

3 tbsp vegan vanilla protein powder

¼ tsp pink salt

⅓ cup honey or pure maple syrup

2½ tbsp coconut oil (melted)

sprinkle of cinnamon

METHOD

1. Preheat oven to 180°C (355°F) and line a large tray with baking paper. Combine all ingredients (except melted coconut oil and honey) in a large bowl and fold together until the protein powder is evenly dispersed

2. Pour melted coconut oil and honey into the mixture and fold through until well combined

3. Transfer the mixture onto the baking tray and flatten out with a spatula. Place in the oven to bake for 9-12 minutes or until golden brown and crispy

4. Remove from the oven and allow the granola to completely cool before breaking into shards and storing in a large glass jar or air tight container

...and perfect for a sneaky snack!

DF   GF   V   VG

FOXY PANCAKES

SERVES 1

INGREDIENTS

1 banana (mashed)

1 large egg

1 tbsp buckwheat flour

¼ tsp cinnamon

1 tsp chia seeds

1 tsp coconut oil (for fry pan)

Suggested Toppings

pure maple syrup

banana

cinnamon

METHOD

1. Add mashed banana, egg, buckwheat flour, cinnamon and chia seeds to a small bowl and whisk together with a fork

2. Heat coconut oil in a fry pan over low heat and pour mixture to create two separate pancakes

3. Cook for 2½ minutes or until bubbles appear on the surface of each pancake then flip and cook the second side for 1 minute

4. Serve with maple syrup, slices of banana and a sprinkle of cinnamon

psst ... kids love them!

DF GF NF VG

MUESLI & YOGHURT CUPS

MAKES 6 CUPS

INGREDIENTS

Muesli Cups

2 cups gluten free rolled oats

½ cup smooth peanut butter

½ cup pure maple syrup

1 tsp vanilla bean paste

¼ tsp pink salt

coconut oil for greasing

Filling

coconut yoghurt

passionfruit pulp

raspberries

METHOD

1. Preheat the oven to 175°C (345°F) and grease a muffin tray with coconut oil

2. Combine all muesli cup ingredients in a bowl and fold together well

3. Evenly distribute mixture into 6 muffin holes and use your fingers to press the base and sides into the hole to create a cup shape

4. Bake in the oven for 15–20 minutes

5. Allow muesli cups to cool before removing them from the muffin tray

6. Fill with coconut yoghurt, passionfruit pulp and raspberries or your desired fillings!

you may need to use a butter knife to pop them out of the holes!

for low FODMAP enjoy no more than two cups and be mindful of toppings as they can be high FODMAP foods in higher quantities

DF   GF   LOW FODMAP   V   VG

MATCHA WAFFLES

MAKES 4-5 WAFFLES

INGREDIENTS

2 large eggs

½ tsp vanilla bean paste

3 tbsp pure maple syrup

1 tsp apple cider vinegar

1 tbsp olive oil

¼ cup nut milk

1 tbsp coconut sugar

1 cup gluten free flour

1 tsp baking powder

1 tsp matcha green tea powder

Topping

pure maple syrup

banana

cacao nibs

this adds a depth of flavour/ toffee undertone to the waffles

METHOD

1. Add eggs, vanilla, maple syrup, apple cider vinegar, olive oil and nut milk to a large bowl and whisk well

2. Add coconut sugar then sift in gluten free flour, baking powder and matcha powder. Fold together until smooth

this will depend on your waffle iron

3. Heat a waffle iron (add a small amount of oil to your iron if necessary) and once heated, add portions of the mixture to your iron and cook for 2-3 minutes or until waffles are fluffy and the surface is golden

4. Transfer fluffy waffles to your serving plate and top with sliced banana, cacao nibs, a drizzle of maple and a sprinkle of coconut sugar and matcha powder!

DF   GF   LOW FODMAP   M·PALEO   VG

ensure your flour is paleo friendly. Coconut sugar is not strictly paleo, but is acceptable as modern paleo in this small amount per serve.

be mindful your toppings are also low FODMAP. enjoy up to 1 waffle

STRAWBERRY & VANILLA CRUNCHY CEREAL

MAKES 1 LARGE JAR

INGREDIENTS

1 cup gluten free rolled oats

½ cup buckwheat groats

1 cup coconut flakes

⅓ cup goji berries

¼ tsp salt

2 tbsp coconut oil (melted)

½ tsp vanilla bean paste

3 tbsp pure maple syrup

1 cup freeze-dried or dehydrated strawberry slices (cut or sliced into smaller pieces)

if your dried strawberries come in larger slices, feel free to use scissors to chop them smaller!

METHOD

1. Preheat oven to 165°C (330°F) and line a large tray with baking paper

2. Add oats, buckwheat groats, coconut flakes, goji berries and salt to a large bowl and mix together well

3. Combine melted coconut oil, vanilla paste and maple syrup together in a small bowl. Whisk together well

4. Pour the wet mixture into the large bowl of dry ingredients and use a rubber cake spatula to fold together well

5. Evenly spread the mixture onto your prepared baking tray and roughly flatten out with the spatula. Place in the oven and bake for 15-20 minutes, remove from the oven at the halfway mark (10 minutes) and toss the cereal around before placing it back into the oven to bake for the remaining 5-10 minutes

6. Remove the crunchy cereal from the oven once the coconut flakes are golden but not burnt. Allow the cereal to cool before scattering your sliced, dried strawberries on top and tossing together with a fork

7. Serve with your favourite plant-based milk like cereal or on top of coconut yoghurt!

make sure you take it out of the oven after 10 minutes and toss the cereal around before placing it back in the oven to cook for the final 10 minutes!

DF GF NF V VG

CURRIED TOFU SCRAMBLE

SERVES 2

INGREDIENTS

250g (8.8oz) firm tofu

1 tsp curry powder

salt & pepper

2 tbsp fresh parsley (finely chopped)

olive oil

4 slices gluten free/paleo bread (toasted)

2 tbsp vegan mayonnaise

1 cup baby spinach

½ avocado

2 tsp dried chilli flakes

METHOD

1. Place your block of tofu in a medium bowl and mash up with a fork

2. Once tofu is scrambled, mix in curry powder, a generous crack of salt and pepper and finely chopped parsley

3. Heat a small amount of olive oil in a large fry pan over medium heat and add tofu scramble to the pan. Use a spatula or wooden spoon to toss the scramble around until it's evenly heated and hot. Meanwhile, toast 4 slices of gluten free bread

4. Transfer tofu scramble back into the medium-sized bowl and combine with vegan mayonnaise. Fold together until evenly combined

5. While the fry pan is still hot, add baby spinach to the pan to lightly wilt

6. Once your toast is ready, use a fork to evenly mash the avocado onto each slice. Top each slice with wilted spinach, curried tofu scramble, a sprinkle of chilli flakes and an extra crack of salt and pepper to taste. So easy, so delicious!

you may need to add a tiny bit of oil

You can also scramble your tofu in a food processor with as little as two pulses/blitzes!

it will have a similar consistency to scrambled eggs

DF   GF   NF   V   VG

34

WARMING BUCKWHEAT PORRIDGE

SERVES 1 LARGE OR 2 SNACK SIZE

INGREDIENTS

½ cup raw buckwheat groats

1 cup almond milk

⅓ cup quick oats

¼ tsp nutmeg

¼ tsp cinnamon

1 cup warm water

2 tbsp pure maple syrup

½ large banana (sliced)

1 tbsp coconut yoghurt (optional)

METHOD

1. Combine buckwheat groats and almond milk in a small saucepan and stir over medium heat. Place the lid ¾ of the way on top (so there's a small space for steam to escape) and stir every few minutes, allowing it to simmer for 10 minutes in total

2. Remove the lid and add quick oats, nutmeg, cinnamon and warm water. Stir well and continue to simmer with the lid off for 10 minutes or until thick and creamy (stir regularly throughout this time)

3. Add 1 tbsp of maple syrup and stir well before serving into 1 or 2 bowls

4. Top with banana, another drizzle of maple syrup, a sprinkle of cinnamon and an optional tablespoon of coconut yoghurt swirled on top. Enjoy warm!

DF · V · VG

MANGO BOOST BOWL

INGREDIENTS

1 large mango (skin & seed removed)

½ cup almond milk

1-2 tsp lime juice

½ tsp vanilla bean paste

¼ cup coconut yoghurt
(or yoghurt of choice)

1 tbsp honey

3 tbsp chia seeds

Topping

shredded coconut

fresh mango

hemp seeds

METHOD

1. Combine mango, almond milk, lime juice, vanilla bean paste, yoghurt and honey in a blender and blend on low until smooth

2. Transfer mango mixture to a medium bowl and whisk in chia seeds. Allow to set in the fridge for 30 minutes – 1 hour

3. Remove from the fridge and serve into two separate bowls along with desired toppings. Enjoy cold!

DF GF VG

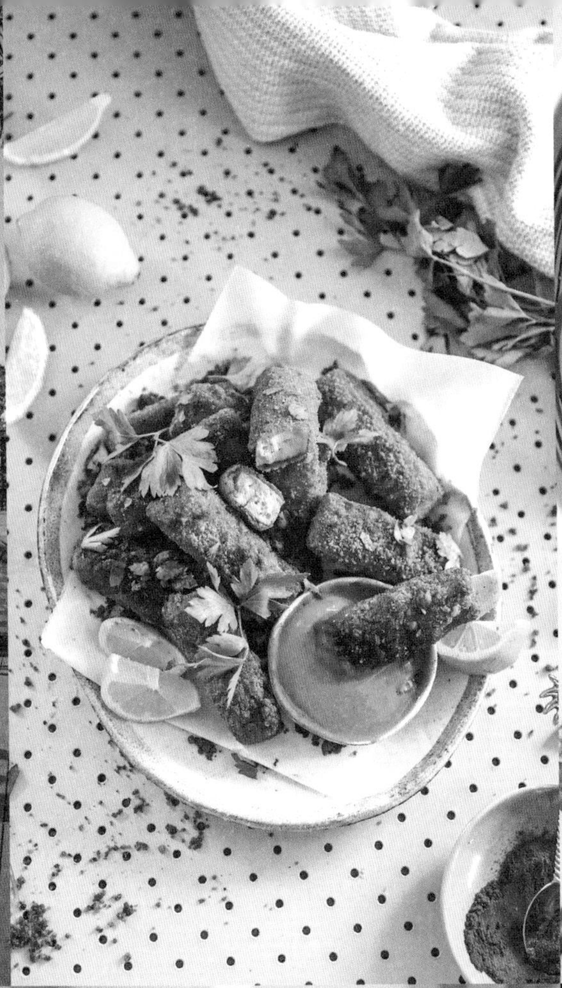

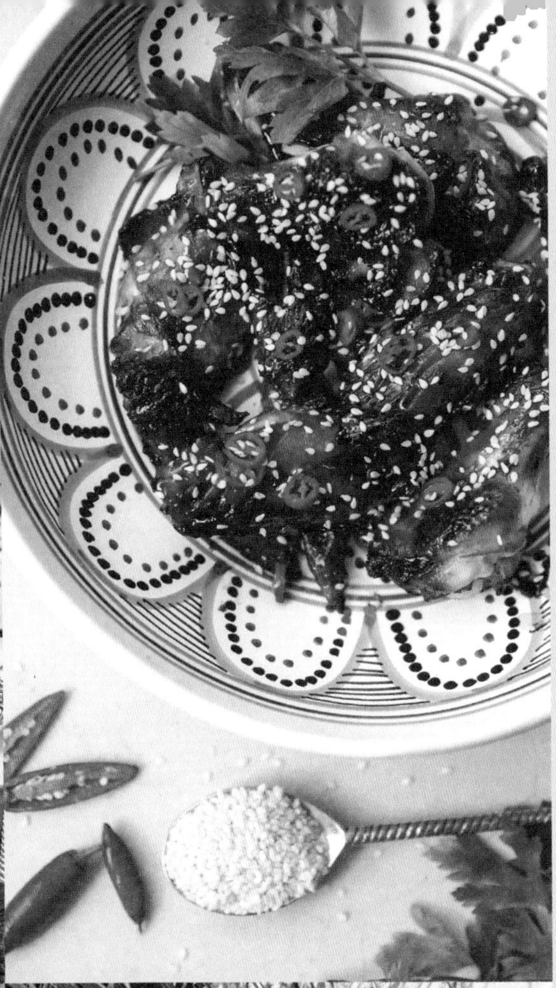

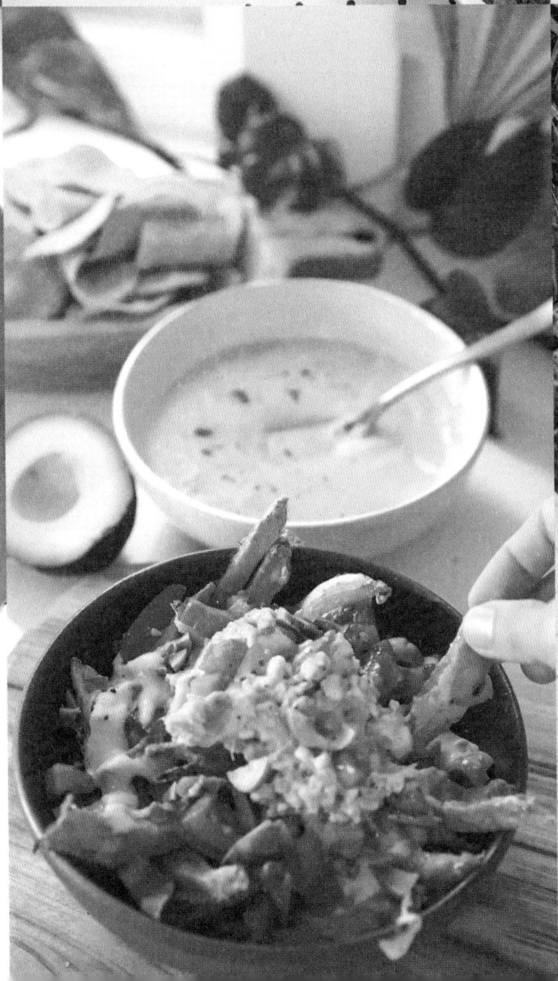

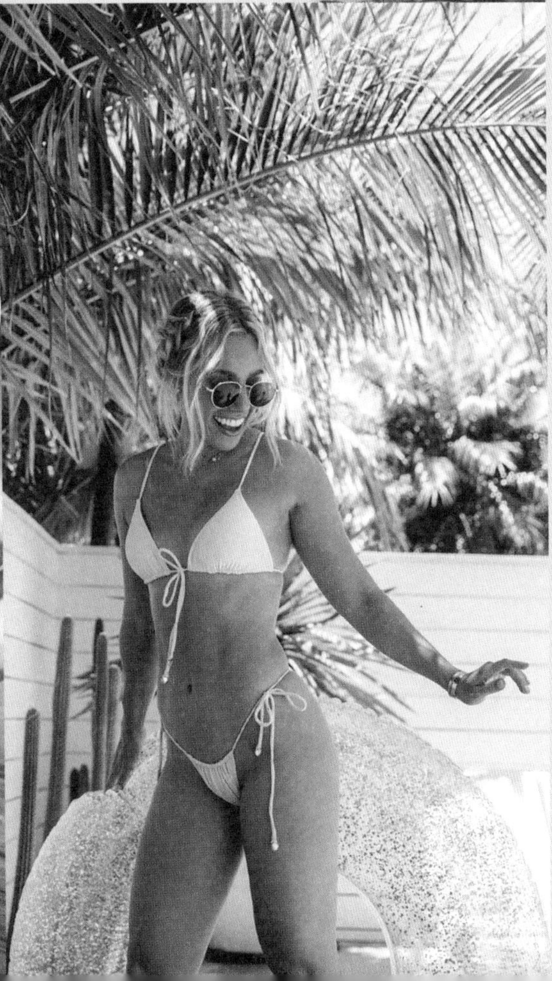

LIGHT MEALS & SIDES

STICKY HONEY CHICKY WINGS

SERVES 4

INGREDIENTS

4 tbsp honey

1 large garlic clove (minced)

4 tbsp tamari

¼ tsp chilli powder

2 tsp olive oil

1kg (2.2lbs) chicken wing nibbles (wingettes/drumettes)

2-3 tsp sesame seeds (for topping)

2-3 bird's eye chillies (finely sliced for topping)

METHOD

1. Combine honey, garlic, tamari, chilli powder and olive oil in a large bowl and whisk together

2. Add chicken wing nibbles to the bowl and toss well in the marinade. Allow to marinate for at least 3 hours or overnight, if possible

3. Preheat the oven to 200°C (395°F) and lightly grease a large tray with olive oil

4. Transfer chicken wing nibbles from the marinade bowl to the tray. Using a pastry brush, lightly brush each wing with more marinade before placing them in the oven to bake for 25 minutes on one side

5. Flip each chicken wing over, brush with any marinade residue and place back into the oven to cook for a further 10 minutes

6. Remove from the oven and top with a sprinkle of sesame seeds and fresh chilli

DF GF M-PALEO NF

THE ULTIMATE SALMON PATTIES

MAKES 8 PATTIES

to ensure it binds well, this needs to be diced so finely that it is almost minced

INGREDIENTS

2 cups (skinless & boneless) salmon (diced)

2 tbsp fresh lemongrass (minced)

2 tsp fresh ginger (minced)

1 tbsp fresh coriander (finely chopped)

2 sprigs fresh dill (finely chopped)

salt & pepper

2 tsp coconut oil

METHOD

1. Add all ingredients (except coconut oil) to a small bowl and mix together

2. Using your hands, scoop out 8 even portions of the mixture and softly press between your palms to form patties

3. Heat 1 tsp of coconut oil in a fry pan over medium heat and add 4 patties to the pan. Cook for 3-4 minutes on each side or until golden brown

4. Remove from heat and set aside, keeping warm. Add the remaining coconut oil and repeat for the remaining 4 patties

5. Serve immediately for lunch/dinner or pack away for meal preps. We like to serve our salmon patties with basmati rice, sprouts and Chia Chilli Jam

see page 229

DF GF LOW FODMAP M-PALEO NF

RAINBOW VEGAN SIZZLE

SERVES 6

INGREDIENTS

Tempeh Sausage Strips

½ tbsp sesame oil

1 garlic clove (minced)

½ tsp gluten free dark soy sauce

1 tbsp tamari

¼ tsp Tabasco sauce
(or more if you like more spice)

¼ tsp onion powder

crack of black pepper

½ tsp coconut sugar

150g (5.3oz) tempeh, sliced into strips
around 2cm wide x 5mm thick (0.8in x 0.2in)

Sizzle Extras

1½ cups purple cabbage (thinly sliced)

½ large lime (juiced)

½ brown onion (thinly sliced)

6 slices gluten free bread

½ tomato (sliced into half moons)

vegan mayonnaise

fresh coriander

METHOD

1. Heat sesame oil in a large fry pan on medium-high heat and swirl it around in the pan so the entire surface is coated

2. Combine garlic, dark soy sauce, tamari, Tabasco sauce, onion powder, black pepper and coconut sugar in a bowl and whisk together well

3. Pour the marinade mixture into the heated pan and immediately place the tempeh strips on top of the marinade

4. Allow the tempeh to cook on one side for 3-4 minutes before flipping over and cook for a further 3 minutes or until all of the marinade liquid has absorbed and tempeh sausage strips begin to crisp and darken in colour. Remove from the pan and set aside

5. Combine thinly sliced purple cabbage and lime juice in a large mason jar. Place the lid on top and shake well, ensuring the lime juice generously coats each strip of cabbage. Allow this to sit for 5-10 minutes to soften the cabbage

6. Add a small drizzle of olive oil over medium heat to the pan used for the tempeh. Once the oil is hot, add in sliced brown onion and sauté until caramelised

7. Warm bread in the microwave or place in the toaster before creating your vegan sizzle and layering lime-infused purple cabbage, tomato, tempeh sausage, caramelised onion, vegan mayo and fresh coriander

DF GF NF V VG

CREAMY POTATO BAKE

SERVES 6-8

INGREDIENTS

Cheesy White Sauce

2 cups raw cashews (soaked in boiling hot water for 1 hour)

2½ cups almond milk

3 garlic cloves

2 tbsp fresh lemon juice

2 tbsp white miso paste

½ cup nutritional yeast

Bake

2 tbsp olive oil

3 brown onions (peeled & finely sliced)

200g (7oz) nitrate-free bacon (finely diced)

1.5kg (3.3lb) white potatoes (washed & sliced)

1 tbsp spring onion (finely chopped)

1 tbsp fresh rosemary (finely chopped)

1 tbsp fresh thyme (finely chopped)

salt & pepper

METHOD

1. Preheat oven to 200°C (395°F) and grease a large ceramic baking dish or lasagne tray with olive oil

2. To prepare the sauce: In a food processor, add pre-soaked cashews, 2 cups of almond milk, garlic, lemon juice, miso and nutritional yeast

3. Blend on a low speed for 2 minutes and increase speed for a further 2 minutes. Check for a smooth and fairly thick consistency then add the final ½ cup of almond milk

4. Blend for a further 2 minutes until the sauce is super smooth

5. To prepare the potato bake: In a medium fry pan, heat olive oil over medium heat then add sliced onions and cook until translucent

6. Remove onions from the pan and set aside. Increase the heat and add bacon to the pan, sauté until lightly golden

7. Evenly slice potatoes to approximately ½cm (0.2in) in thickness

8. In a large bowl add onion, bacon, spring onion, rosemary, thyme, salt, pepper and cheesy white sauce. Using a spatula, gently fold all ingredients together

9. Using a large ladle, scoop out 2 ladles' worth of the cheesy bacon mixture and place in a small bowl for later. This will be the topping of our potato bake

10. Using your hands, add potatoes to the remaining cheesy bacon mix and toss well so potatoes are evenly coated

11. In your prepared baking dish, roughly layer the slices of potato on top of one another. Once all slices of potato are in the dish, drizzle the 2 ladles of cheesy bacon mixture on top. Use a rubber cake spatula to smooth out the surface and cover all slices of potato

12. Cover with foil and place in the preheated oven for 40 minutes

13. Decrease oven temperature to 130°C (265°F), remove the foil and continue to cook for a further 30-40 minutes

DF GF

TURNIP FRIES

SERVES 2

if you like yours crispy leave in the oven for an extra 3-5 minutes

INGREDIENTS

1 tbsp avocado oil (spray works best)

4 turnips (washed, peeled, & cut into matchsticks)

2 tbsp arrowroot flour

1 sprig fresh rosemary (stem removed & finely chopped)

1 tsp dried parsley (chopped)

½ tsp smoked paprika

½ tsp onion powder

½ tsp garlic powder

1 tsp pink salt flakes + more for serving

METHOD

1. Preheat oven to 220°C (430°F) and spray a wire rack with avocado oil

2. Place turnip matchsticks (fries) into a large bowl and coat with avocado oil

3. In a small bowl combine arrowroot, rosemary, parsley, paprika, onion and garlic powder, salt and mix well

4. Sprinkle the spice mix over turnips and toss to coat evenly

5. Lay turnip fries evenly out on your prepared wire rack and bake in a preheated oven for 15 minutes

6. Once fries are cooked to your liking, remove and sprinkle with extra salt. Serve immediately

DF GF M-PALEO NF V VG

GAME DAY TOFU STICKS

MAKES 12 STICKS

INGREDIENTS

¾ cup gluten free breadcrumbs

salt & pepper

¼ tsp ground cumin

1 tsp garlic powder

2 tsp sweet paprika

½ tsp onion powder

1 cup coconut milk

1 cup tapioca flour

1 block (500g/1.1lb) firm tofu (cut lengthways into strips)

METHOD

1. Preheat oven to 200°C (395°F) and line a baking tray with baking paper

2. Combine gluten free breadcrumbs, salt, pepper, cumin, garlic powder, paprika and onion powder in a small bowl and mix well

3. Pour coconut milk into one bowl and tapioca flour into a separate bowl

4. With one hand coat all 4 sides of the tofu stick in tapioca flour then place tofu stick into coconut milk, coat and remove with a fork. With a clean fork, place tofu stick in the breadcrumb mix and coat evenly

5. Place onto a lined baking tray and repeat until all 12 tofu sticks are crumbed

6. Bake for 10 minutes and flip each stick then bake for a further 10 minutes. Serve with Buffalo Sauce or gluten free sweet chilli sauce!

see page 58

DF GF NF V VG

LOADED MEXI SWEET POTATO FRIES

SERVES 1

INGREDIENTS

3 small sweet potatoes (peeled)

2 tbsp tapioca starch

½ tsp onion powder

¼ tsp garlic powder

¼ tsp smoked paprika

olive oil

pink salt

½ avocado (mashed)

½ tbsp lime juice

generous drizzle (around ¼ cup) vegan Nacho Cheeze

½ large tomato (diced)

¼ cup Sicilian olives (finely sliced)

see page 233

METHOD

1. Slice sweet potatoes into large fries, around 9cm (3.5in) long and 1cm (0.4in) wide

2. Place sweet potato fries in a large bowl and cover with cold water. Ensure all of the slices are completely submerged. Allow the sweet potato to soak in the water for a few hours (30 minutes minimum)

3. Preheat the oven to 210°C (410°F) and line two large baking trays with baking paper

4. While you soak your sweet potato fries, prepare Nacho Cheeze

5. Drain the water from the sweet potato and place slices on a linen tea towel. Use a separate tea towel to press down on the sweet potato and completely dry each slice. Once dried, lay out slices on a work surface

6. Combine tapioca starch, onion powder, garlic powder and smoked paprika in a small bowl and mix together

7. Sprinkle tapioca mix over the sweet potato slices, ensuring each side is covered and well-coated in the mix

8. Drizzle a generous amount of olive oil over the tapioca-coated slices and toss well. Ensure there are no dry patches of tapioca starch left on the sweet potato, each needs to be lightly coated in the oil

9. Lay the sweet potato slices onto your prepared baking trays, ensuring that no slices are overlapping or touch one another then place in the oven, and bake for 20 minutes

10. Remove from the oven after 20 minutes, flip each slice and return to the oven for a further 10 minutes. Your fries should be golden

11. Remove sweet potato fries from the oven and generously season with pink salt then place fries in a serving bowl

12. Combine mashed avocado and lime juice together in a small bowl

13. Top sweet potato fries with vegan Nacho Cheeze, mashed avocado, diced tomato, sliced olives, and serve hot!

DF GF V VG

CRISPY BAKED
CHICKY NUGGETS

MAKES 18-20 NUGGETS

INGREDIENTS

Chicken Mixture

500g (1.1lb) chicken breast mince

¼ tsp garlic powder

¼ tsp salt

¼ cup gluten free flour

Coating

2 large eggs

⅓ cup gluten free flour (or any flour)

Crumbing

¾ cup gluten free breadcrumbs or rice crumbs

½ tsp garlic powder

1 tsp pink salt

½ tsp sweet paprika

½ tsp onion powder

avocado oil spray (or olive oil spray)

METHOD

1. Preheat oven to 180°C (355°F) and line a baking tray with baking paper

2. Add chicken mixture ingredients to a large bowl and mix together well

3. Crack eggs into a medium-sized bowl and whisk together. Place gluten free flour onto a large plate

4. Add all crumbing ingredients to a separate plate and toss together well

5. To create the chicken nugget shapes, use two identical metal tablespoons and <u>quenelle</u> the mixture. (don't overdo it as the chicken mince will become too sticky)

scoop out a heaped tablespoon worth of chicken mince in one of the spoons. Pass the chicken mince repeatedly between the spoons, turning and smoothing each side until a neat quenelle or oval-shaped nugget has formed!

DF GF NF

53

6. One by one, place chicken mince nuggets onto the plate of flour. Use a separate spoon to help roll the nugget around, ensuring the entire outside is coated in flour

7. Gently transfer the flour-coated nugget to the egg mixture and with another fresh spoon roll it around until the egg has coated the nugget

8. Use a small, slotted spoon or fork to <u>pick up</u> the <u>nugget from</u> the egg mixture (allowing any excess egg to drain through the spoon/fork) and transfer to the crumbing plate. Use a fresh fork to roll the nugget around in the crumbing until evenly and well coated. Place the crumbed chicken nugget onto the prepared baking tray

scoop up the nugget, do not stab it!

9. Repeat this process for the entire mixture to create 18-20 nuggets

10. Once all chicken nuggets have been crumbed and placed on the baking tray, spray an even layer of avocado or olive oil over the top of each nugget (this is much easier to do with a spray oil) and place in the oven to bake for 25 minutes

11. Remove from the oven and serve with your favourite side salad, lemon wedges, tomato sauce, sweet chilli sauce or tomato chutney!

CRISPY MAPLE TOFU WEDGES

SERVES 4

INGREDIENTS

450g (16oz) firm tofu

4 tbsp arrowroot flour

2 tbsp sesame oil

2 tbsp pure maple syrup

1½ tbsp tamari

METHOD

removing as much excess water as possible will help make your wedges crispy!

1. Rinse tofu and <u>firmly pat dry</u> with a paper towel or a linen tea towel and cut into triangle wedges (around 20 pieces)

2. Pour arrowroot flour onto a plate and one by one, roll tofu triangles in the arrowroot flour until completely coated

3. Heat sesame oil in a large fry pan or wok over medium-high heat and add tofu wedges

4. Cook wedges evenly on each side until they're golden and crispy. This will take a few minutes on each side

make these into lettuce cups! see page 112

5. Drizzle maple syrup and tamari into the pan/wok once tofu is crispy. Reduce heat to low-medium and continuously stir liquid through the tofu wedges, gently folding together to coat each wedge. Continue to fold through and heat until all the liquid has been absorbed and reduced, this will leave you with a crispy, sticky tofu!

6. Add crispy maple tofu wedges to your fave nourish bowl, inside a <u>lettuce cup</u> with vermicelli noodles or add to a simple stir-fry!

DF GF LOW FODMAP NF V VG

EASTERN CHICKEN

SERVES 3

INGREDIENTS

2 chicken breasts, cut into 1.5cm (0.6in) cubes

10 sprigs fresh thyme (stem removed)

2 garlic cloves (minced)

2 tbsp coconut yoghurt

1 tsp tomato paste

1½ tsp sweet paprika

2 tsp olive oil

1 tsp pink salt

METHOD

1. Combine all ingredients to a bowl (except chicken) and mix well to form the marinade

2. Add diced chicken to marinade and coat well with a spoon

3. Cover the bowl and place in the fridge for at least 1 hour to allow chicken to absorb the flavours

4. Preheat oven to 180°C (355°F) and line a baking tray with baking paper. Place chicken on the tray ensuring there is space between each piece

5. Once oven is preheated bake the chicken for 12 minutes

6. Add chicken to pre-made salads, wraps or sandwiches for the perfect hit of protein for your homemade lunch or dinner!

to check if chicken is cooked, take what looks like the thickest or biggest piece and cut into it using a knife. the juices should be clear and the flesh of the chicken white

DF   GF   M-PALEO   NF

56

SMOKEY BUFFALO WINGS

SERVES 4-5 AS A SIDE

INGREDIENTS

Wings

1kg (2.2lbs) chicken wing nibbles
(wingettes/drumettes)

2 tsp baking powder

pink salt

Buffalo Sauce

2 tbsp vegan butter

¼ cup Frank's hot sauce (or hot sauce
of choice)

¼ tsp smokey Tabasco

1 tbsp coconut sugar

1 tsp apple cider vinegar

pink salt

Fresh Dippy Sauce

¼ cup coconut yoghurt

¼ tsp nutritional yeast

pink salt

⅛ tsp garlic powder

¼ tsp fresh lime juice

METHOD

1. Preheat oven to 120°C (250°F) and line a
   baking tray with foil

2. Pat wings dry and remove any excess
   moisture with a paper towel

3. Add chicken, baking powder and a pinch
   of salt to a large bowl and toss together
   until evenly coated

4. Place wings evenly onto a lined baking
   tray and bake in the oven for 30 minutes

5. Increase oven temperature to 220°C
   (430°F) and bake for a further 40 minutes

6. Meanwhile, in a small saucepan over
   low-medium heat, prepare the Buffalo
   Sauce by melting vegan butter. Once
   melted, add all ingredients and whisk
   until combined

7. For the Fresh Dippy Sauce, combine all
   ingredients in a small bowl, mix together
   and set aside in the fridge until wings are
   ready to serve

8. Remove wings and carefully place into
   a bowl. Pour over the desired amount of
   Buffalo Sauce and toss together well

9. Plate with Fresh Dippy Sauce and enjoy!

feel free to use clean hands here to toss your chicken!

DF GF NF

MUSHROOM ARANCINI BALLS

MAKES 24

INGREDIENTS

Mushroom Risotto Filling

2 tbsp olive oil

1 red onion (finely diced)

1 garlic clove (minced)

4 large portobello mushrooms (finely chopped)

2 cups arborio rice

½ cup water

2 cups gluten free vegetable stock

2 tsp thyme (finely chopped)

1 tbsp nutritional yeast

salt & pepper

Crumb mix

1¼ cups gluten free breadcrumbs

1 tbsp nutritional yeast

4 tbsp tapioca flour

1 cup almond milk

½ cup olive oil

METHOD

1. Heat 2 tbsp of olive oil in a medium saucepan over medium heat and add onions. Sauté for 1 minute before adding garlic and cooking for a further minute

2. Add mushrooms to the saucepan and combine well with onions and garlic, stirring for 1-2 minutes

3. Add arborio rice to the saucepan and cook for 2 minutes stirring continuously. Add ½ cup of water and stir until absorbed

4. Add in ¼ cup of vegetable stock and stir until fully absorbed. Repeat this process, adding ¼ cups of stock until fully absorbed and there is no stock remaining

5. Add thyme, nutritional yeast, salt, pepper and stir

6. When all the liquid has been absorbed, the rice should be tender and creamy (approximately 25 minutes)

7. Spread the risotto onto a baking tray and place it in the fridge to cool

8. In 3 separate bowls, place breadcrumbs and nutritional yeast in the first and stir well. In the second, place tapioca flour and in the third, almond milk

9. Once the rice has cooled, take spoonfuls of the rice mixture and roll into balls

10. Place a ball into tapioca flour and coat well, then place into the milk and then using a fork, place into breadcrumbs, ensuring to coat each ball well

11. Repeat this process until all of the mixture has been made into crumbed balls

12. In a small saucepan, heat ½ cup of olive oil on medium heat. Once the oil is hot, place 3 balls at a time into saucepan and shallow-fry on one side until golden brown. Once golden, rotate the balls around, allowing them to cook evenly on the other side (you will have to rotate the balls in the hot oil so they cook evenly on all sides)

13. Remove mushroom arancini balls from the saucepan and place them on a piece of paper towel to absorb any excess oil.

14. Sprinkle a little salt on top before serving as the perfect starter or canapé!

your oil is too hot if it starts spitting at you. the oil should bubble and sizzle once the balls have been submerged and begin to cook

use your hands here!

ensure the balls don't overlap!

DF GF NF V VG

To bake in oven:

(keep in mind — these don't turn out as golden and crispy as when they're shallow fried)

1. Preheat oven to 180°C (355°F)

2. Coat balls and place on a lined baking tray

3. Place in preheated oven for 20 minutes, turning halfway through cooking time.

TEMPEH TEMPTERS

MAKES 4-5 SKEWERS

300g (10.5oz) organic tempeh

2 tbsp coconut aminos

1 tbsp fresh lime juice

1 tbsp pure maple syrup

pink salt (to taste)

1 tbsp coconut oil

5 bamboo skewers

Suggested Toppings

sesame seeds

fresh red chilli (finely sliced)

1. Soak bamboo skewers in water and set aside for later

2. Cut tempeh into 2cm (0.8in) cubes and place in a medium-sized bowl along with coconut aminos, lime, maple syrup and a few cracks of pink salt. Fold gently together so each cube is soaked with the marinade.
   If you have time to cover this and set in the fridge to marinate for a few hours, that's ideal!

3. Remove bamboo skewers from the water, pat dry with a tea towel. Thread around 4-5 cubes of tempeh onto each skewer

4. Heat coconut oil in a large fry pan over medium heat and cook skewers for around 1-2 minutes each side or until they're a deep golden colour and lightly charred. We like to pour the rest of the marinade over the skewers while cooking for maximum flavour!

5. Sprinkle sesame seeds and fresh chilli on top to serve

all four sides!

be careful not to let the syrup burn! you may need to turn your heat down and rotate skewers frequently around the excess marinade in the pan!

we suggest serving with roasted vegetables or healthy fried rice for a main meal

DF GF NF V VG

SEASIDE COCONUT SCALLOPS

MAKES 6

INGREDIENTS

2 tbsp coconut oil

½ bird's eye chilli (seeds removed & finely minced)

1 tsp minced garlic

½ tsp freshly ground black pepper

6 scallops in the shell

1 tbsp dry white wine

¼ bunch flat-leaf parsley leaves (picked & torn)

lemon wedges to serve

METHOD

1. Melt the coconut oil in a small pan on low-medium heat, add the chilli and garlic to the pan with the black pepper. Combine well and set aside for at least 1 hour before cooking the scallops

2. Heat your barbecue to medium-high heat. Place the shells with the scallops inside them on a plate. Pour a small amount of white wine onto each scallop and using tongs, place the shells onto the barbecue. Cover with the lid for 2 minutes, the scallops should turn an opaque colour

3. Flip over for a further minute or until the grill marks are on the scallop

4. Remove scallops and drizzle the coconut oil mixture over each scallop and scatter with torn parsley, enjoy!

dry white wine is not strictly paleo

DF GF M·PALEO NF

CAULIFLOWER TORTILLAS

MAKES 6-8 TORTILLAS

see page 8

INGREDIENTS

2 cups cauliflower rice uncooked

2 eggs

2 tbsp coconut flour

1 cup tapioca starch

½ tsp salt

1 tsp garlic powder

1 cup almond milk

2 tbsp avocado oil

METHOD

1. Microwave cauliflower rice for 3 minutes. Remove rice from the microwave and transfer into a milk bag to wring out any excess water.

2. Add drained cauliflower rice, egg, coconut flour, tapioca starch, salt, garlic powder and ¾ cup almond milk to a blender. Blend for 3-4 minutes or until a smooth consistency is achieved. Add in remaining almond milk until combined

3. Heat avocado oil in a large fry pan and scoop ⅓ cup-sized portions of the cauli batter to your fry pan. Each tortilla needs to be thin so be sure to pour evenly and rotate the pan to get a crêpe-like shape

4. Flip when slightly golden. Once both sides have slightly browned (after 2-4 minutes), remove tortilla from pan and repeat the process until no batter remains

5. These tortillas pair perfectly with our Coconut Tzatziki and your protein of choice or our Pineapple Pulled Pork Tacos

see page 229

see page 158

if your batter is runny use slightly less

if you don't have a milk bag then you can press the heated cauliflower rice into the centre of a thin tea towel, pull all corners of the towel together and twist to wring out the cauliflower

DF GF VG

PROSCIUTTO-WRAPPED MEATBALLS

MAKES 15 MEATBALLS

INGREDIENTS

500g (1.1lb) grass-fed beef mince

1 large egg

½ brown onion (finely diced)

1 garlic clove (minced)

1 tsp sweet paprika

⅓ cup fresh parsley (finely chopped)

2 tbsp buckwheat flour

2 tsp olive oil

1 tsp ground cumin

1 red chilli (finely sliced)

100g (3.5oz) prosciutto or 8 slices
(cut in half lengthways)

Serving Suggestion

Coconut Tzatziki ⟶ *see page 229*

METHOD

1. Preheat oven to 175°C (345°F) and line a large tray with baking paper

2. Combine all ingredients (except prosciutto) in a large bowl and use a fork or your hands to mix together well

3. Use a spring-loaded ice cream scooper or tablespoon to scoop out 15 even meatballs from the mixture and gently compress together with your hands to form a meatball

4. Ensure you have cut the prosciutto slices in half lengthways so each slice is around 2-3cm (0.8-1.2in) wide. Use one sliced prosciutto ribbon per meatball, wrapping it around the outside so it overlaps by a few centimetres from end to end

5. Place prosciutto-wrapped meatballs in the oven for 20-25 minutes

6. Serve with Coconut Tzatziki and your favourite side salad!

Place the meatball on top of the prosciutto and lap-over to help it stay together

DF GF NF

QUICK DILL & CHICKEN MEATBALLS

MAKES 12 MEATBALLS

INGREDIENTS

500g (1.1lb) minced chicken breast

2 garlic cloves (minced)

2 heaped tbsp fresh dill (finely chopped)

2 tbsp whole egg mayonnaise

3 tbsp buckwheat flour

½ tsp pink salt

METHOD

1. Preheat oven to 175°C (345°F) and prepare a large tray with baking paper

2. Combine all ingredients in a large bowl and mash together using a fork (or combine in a food processor)

3. Using a small <u>ice cream scooper,</u> scoop out 12 even balls and place onto your prepared baking tray

4. Bake in the oven for 17 minutes (flip each meatball at the 10-minute mark) or until <u>lightly golden</u>

5. Serve with your favourite Sunee side or store in an airtight container in the fridge and use for meal preps or nourish bowls on demand

mixture will be sticky so don't use your hands, alternatively you can use a spoon!

don't leave them too long as they will dry out!

DF GF NF

69

CHICKEN SATAY SKEWERS

MAKES 6 SKEWERS

INGREDIENTS

800g (1.7lb) chicken tenderloins (cut into chunks)

½ cup canned coconut milk

2 garlic cloves (minced)

¼ tsp ginger (finely grated)

2½ tsp tamari

1 tsp coconut sugar

¼ tsp ground coriander

¼ tsp ground cumin

¼ tsp turmeric powder

¼ tsp fresh lime juice

⅛ tsp Thai red curry paste

6 long bamboo skewers

Serving Suggestion

Chefy Satay Sauce

see Page 236

METHOD

1. Combine all ingredients (except chicken) in a large bowl and stir well

2. Add chicken to the marinade and stir to ensure all chicken is evenly coated

3. Cover and place in the refrigerator for a minimum of 2 hours (leave overnight for the best result)

4. Preheat the oven to 180°C (355°F) and line a baking tray with baking paper

5. Thread chicken onto bamboo skewers evenly

6. Place onto your prepared baking tray and bake in preheated oven for 14 minutes (or until chicken is cooked but still juicy)

7. Remove from the oven and serve with Chefy Satay Sauce, rice, cauliflower rice or our Chicken Satay Nourish Bowl!

see Page 104

be sure not to bunch up chicken so that it cooks correctly

DF GF

72

SWEET & CRISPY BEEF LETTUCE CUPS

SERVES 4-6

INGREDIENTS

Sweet Beef

drizzle of olive oil

½ small red onion (finely diced)

500g (1.1lb) beef mince

¼ tsp salt

¾ tsp ground coriander

250g (0.5lb) canned water chestnut slices (drained & rinsed)

1 tbsp tamari

1½ tbsp coconut sugar

½ tbsp lime juice

Lettuce Cups

½ Lebanese cucumber (finely cut into matchsticks)

½ cup fresh coriander leaves

dried chilli flakes

4–6 iceberg lettuce cups (washed well)

METHOD

1. Heat a drizzle of olive oil in a large fry pan over medium-high heat

2. Once the oil is hot, sauté the onion until soft then add beef mince, salt and ground coriander. Toss well until the beef is almost cooked through and brown

3. Add remaining sweet beef ingredients to the fry pan and toss together well then take off the heat

4. Assemble the lettuce cups with all components, sprinkling dried chilli on top to serve

taste test and add salt or more lime juice to your liking

DF GF M.PALEO

75

SUNEE SAUSAGE ROLLS

MAKES 12 ROLLS

INGREDIENTS

2 sheets gluten free puff pastry

1 tsp olive oil

1 stalk celery (finely sliced)

500g (1.1lb) high-quality gluten free sausage mince

½ cup brown onion (finely diced)

1 carrot (peeled & grated)

½ cup tightly packed baby spinach (finely sliced)

2 garlic cloves (minced)

1 tbsp tomato paste

1 tbsp gluten free Worcestershire sauce

1 tsp dried mixed herbs

2 eggs

2 tsp seeded mustard (optional)

1 tsp sesame seeds (optional)

METHOD

1. Preheat oven to 180°C (355°F) and line a baking tray with baking paper

2. Take the 2 sheets of puff pastry out of the freezer and place on a benchtop, cover with a damp tea towel to prevent pastry from drying out while thawing

3. In a small pan, add oil and heat on medium heat. Add celery and fry until just cooked then set aside to cool

4. Add mince, onion, carrot, baby spinach, garlic, tomato paste, Worcestershire, herbs, 1 egg and the cooled celery to a large bowl and combine well

5. Once your pastry sheets have thawed out, take one sheet and place onto a piece of baking paper. Using a rolling pin, roll out the pastry on all four sides so that it is a little thinner

6. Using a knife, cut the pastry in half, take one half and if using mustard, spread this down the centre of the piece. Divide your meat mixture into quarters and take a quarter and place this on top of your mustard line. If not using mustard, place the sausage mixture down the centre of your pastry. Be sure to spread evenly and go right to each end of the pastry

7. Crack the second egg into a small bowl and whisk. This is your egg wash. Using your pastry brush or your fingers, brush one side of the pastry with your beaten egg wash. Fold the side that has no egg wash over the meat first and then fold the side with the egg wash over on top, making sure they overlap. Take a fork and gently press the pastry fold onto each other so they stick together

8. Flip the roll over and cut into 3 even pieces. Take your fork again and dip it into your egg wash, prick the tops so that the heat can escape when cooking

9. Brush the tops of the rolls with egg wash and sprinkle with sesame seeds

10. Place rolls on a prepared tray and place in your preheated oven for 35 minutes. Enjoy hot!

DF GF NF

LOADED PESTO TOASTIE

SERVES 2

roughly 1 sweet potato

INGREDIENTS

8 discs of <u>sweet potato r</u>ounds (thinly sliced)

2 tbsp olive oil

crack of salt

1 carrot (peeled & thinly sliced)

1 tsp raw honey

4 slices of gluten free bread (or bread of choice)

½ tbsp vegan butter

1 tbsp <u>Basil Pesto</u> — *see page 235*

½ avocado

1 tomato (sliced)

½ cup rocket

2 tbsp goat's feta

salt & pepper

METHOD

1. Preheat oven to 180°C (355°F) and line a tray with baking paper

2. Add sweet potato to a bowl and evenly cover with 1 tbsp olive oil and a pinch of salt. Lay the sweet potato on the baking tray and place in the preheated oven. Cook for 30-40 minutes, checking with a fork to test if they are soft. Once cooked, remove from oven and set aside

3. Add carrot, remaining oil and honey to a small saucepan. Cook on medium heat until the carrot is soft and tender. Remove from the heat and set aside to cool

4. Lay 4 pieces of bread on a chopping board and spread vegan butter on each piece

5. On 2 pieces, spread the Basil Pesto and on the other 2 pieces, spread the avocado

6. Layer the carrot over the avocado and the sweet potato over the pesto. Place the tomato on top of the sweet potato slices and top with rocket

7. Crumble goat's feta over the rocket and season with salt and pepper

8. Press the two slices of gluten free bread together and place in a preheated sandwich press, toast to your liking!

GF NF

THE GF BASE

MAKES 4 MEDIUM PIZZA BASES

INGREDIENTS

1¼ cups warm water

1 tbsp instant dried yeast

1 tbsp honey

1 tsp salt

1 tbsp psyllium husk

2½ cups plain gluten free flour

½ cup blanched almond meal

2 tsp xanthan gum *we like oregano and basil*

1 tsp dried herbs (optional)

¼ cup extra virgin olive oil (+ extra for greasing)

METHOD

1. Combine warm water, yeast, honey, salt and psyllium husk in a bowl and whisk together well. Set aside in a warm place to activate for 10-15 minutes

2. Combine flour, almond meal and xanthan gum in a separate bowl and mix together (option to add dried herbs here)

3. Pour the olive oil into your now-foamy, wet mixture and whisk. Transfer into the bowl with your dry ingredients

4. Use the dough hook inserts on your electric hand mixer (or use a stand mixer with a dough paddle) and mix on low speed for 8 minutes until thick and sticky

5. Gently scrape the dough out onto a work surface and roll/knead the dough 2-4 times to form a smooth round ball

you may need to add a little olive oil to your hands if your dough is a little too sticky for this

6. Drizzle olive oil into your bowl and swirl it around until well coated

7. Place your dough into the bowl, cover with plastic wrap/tea towel and set aside in a warm place for 2 hours (or longer if possible). Once your dough has rested it will have risen and become fluffy

8. Preheat the oven to 200°C (395°F) fan-forced and place 2 large trays in the oven to get hot

9. Transfer the dough to a clean work surface and cut into four even pieces

10. Knead each piece a few times until the dough is smooth and bouncy

11. Place a large sheet of baking paper on your work surface and put one of your balls of dough in the centre. Using a rolling pin, roll out the dough into a thin circle (around 25cm/10in wide)

12. Remove the hot tray from the oven and set aside. Brush the surface of the pizza base with olive oil then holding each side of the baking paper, flip the pizza base onto the hot tray so the olive oil side is touching the tray

13. Parbake in the oven for 5-7 minutes. Repeat these steps for the remaining 3 balls of dough or tightly wrap the remaining balls of dough in plastic wrap and freeze for another day

14. Allow your pizza base to cool before adding your sauce and toppings of choice and baking in the oven for around 10 minutes (or as crispy as you like it)

you may want to sprinkle a bit of flour on your hands and work surface

DF GF V

SPICY CHICKPEAS

SERVES 1

INGREDIENTS

1 can chickpeas (drained & rinsed)

1 tsp olive oil

1 tsp ground cumin

½ tsp chilli powder

½ tsp paprika

½ tsp pink salt

METHOD

1. Preheat oven to 220°C (430°F) and line a tray with baking paper

2. Dry the chickpeas using a paper towel, you can remove the skins for crunchier chickpeas

3. Add all ingredients to a bowl and toss together well

4. Spread evenly on prepared baking tray and bake for 25 minutes

5. Serve by themselves or with our Tandoori Prawn Skewer Bowl

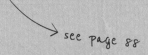

see page 88

for low FODMAP enjoy up to 1/4 of a cup

DF   GF   LOW FODMAP   NF   V   VG

SALADS & NOURISH BOWLS

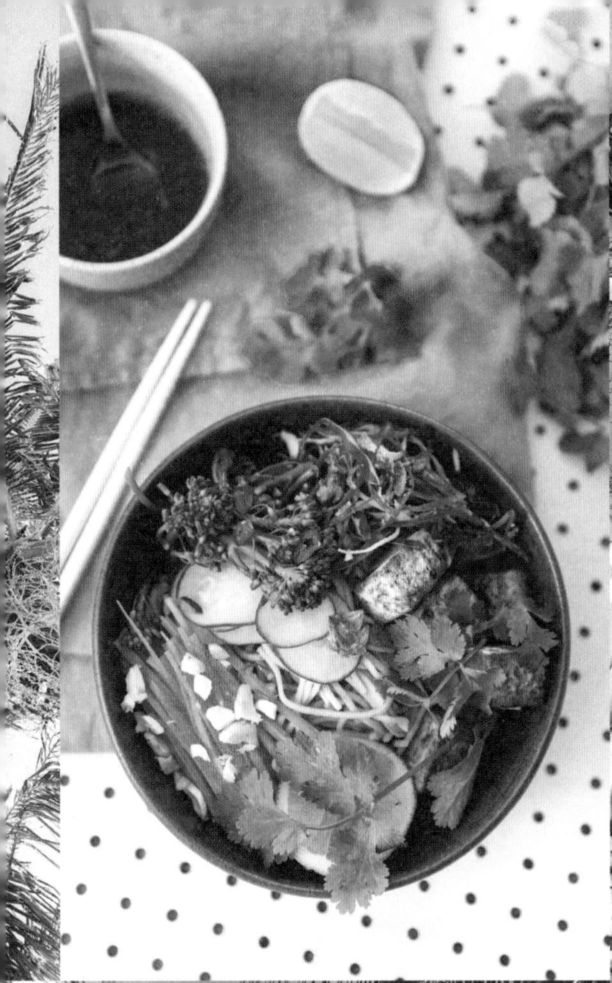

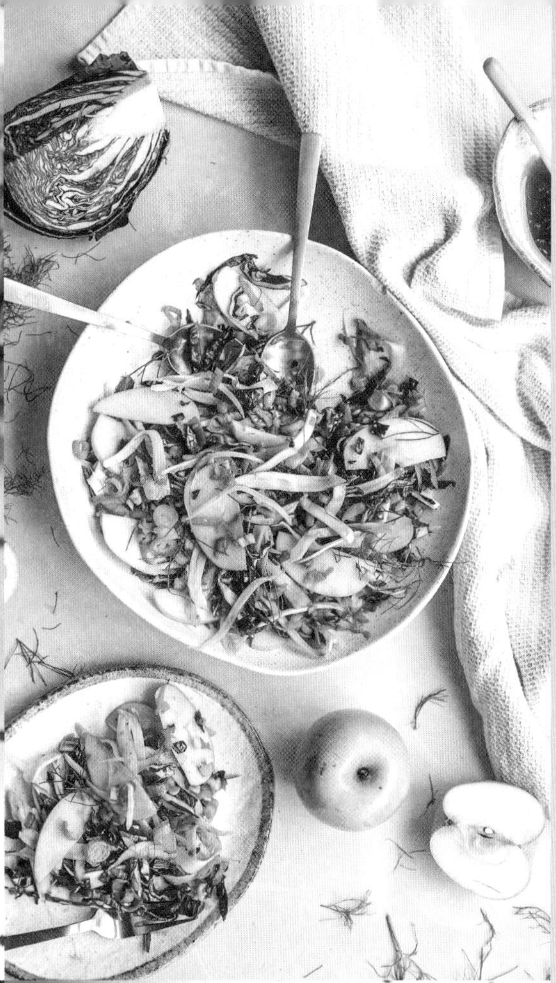

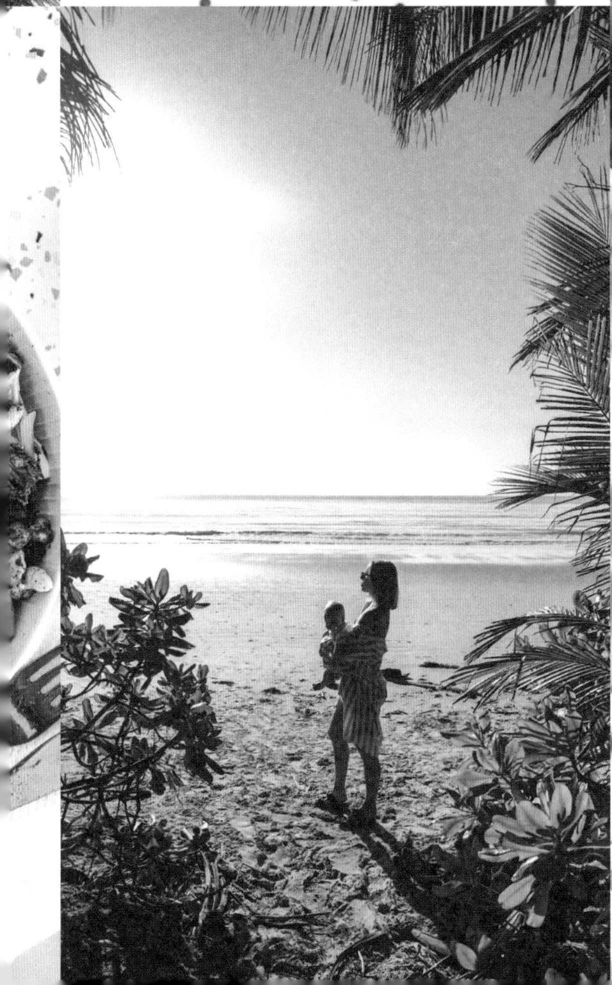

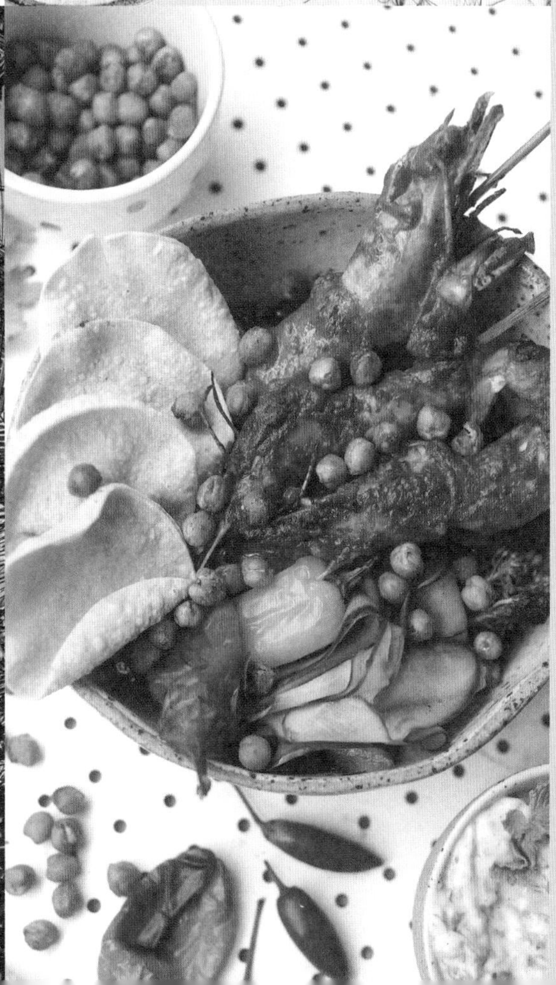

SHREDDY MANGO & CHICKEN SALAD

SERVES 4

see page 9

INGREDIENTS

1 large chicken breast (poached & shredded)

1 large mango (diced)

½ red onion (finely diced)

1 red chilli (deseeded & finely diced)

3 cups iceberg lettuce (shredded/sliced)

2 cups baby spinach

½ Lebanese cucumber (diced)

¼ cup coriander leaves and stems (finely chopped)

¼ cup fresh mint leaves (whole or roughly chopped)

½ large avocado (sliced in crescent moons)

Dressing

3 tbsp lime juice

2 tbsp coconut sugar

1½ tsp fish sauce

1 tbsp sesame oil

2 tsp sweet chilli sauce (optional)

METHOD

1. Poach chicken breast. Once cool, shred using two forks or a food processor

2. Add all salad ingredients to a large serving bowl and gently toss together

3. Combine all dressing ingredients together in a small bowl and whisk together

4. Drizzle dressing over the top of the salad and toss together gently before serving

DF   GF   M-PALEO   NF

85

TANDOORI PRAWN SKEWER BOWL

SERVES 2

INGREDIENTS

6 large green prawns (shells removed & deveined)

Tandoori Marinade

1 tsp olive oil

½ tsp ground coriander

½ tsp ground cumin

½ tsp cayenne pepper

1½ tsp garam masala

½ tsp sweet paprika

¼ cup coconut yoghurt

juice from ½ a lemon

1 garlic clove (minced)

¼ tsp pink salt

7 bamboo skewers

Bowl

1 cup uncooked black rice

8 baby capsicums

8 stems broccolini (steamed)

½ cucumber (peeled into ribbons)

Spicy Chickpeas

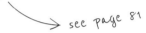 see page 81

Raita

1 cucumber (diced & liquid removed)

1 tbsp fresh coriander

1 lime (juiced)

4 mint leaves (chopped)

¼ tsp ground coriander

¼ tsp ground cumin

pinch of nutmeg

pinch of cinnamon

¼ cup coconut yoghurt

METHOD

1. Combine all marinade ingredients in a small bowl and mix well

2. Toss the shelled and deveined prawns through marinade until evenly coated. Cover the bowl and place in the fridge to marinate for 6-8 hours

3. Add all raita ingredients to a small bowl and stir until evenly combined (or blitz in a food processor)

4. Prepare black rice as per packet instructions

5. Preheat oven to 200°C (395°F) and line 2 baking trays with baking paper

6. Remove prawns from the fridge and thread onto bamboo skewers

7. Place baby capsicums onto one prepared baking tray and prawn skewers on the other baking tray

8. Place into the preheated oven, bake capsicums for 10 minutes and prawn skewers for 15 minutes

9. Add the rice, broccolini, capsicums, cucumber, prawn skewers and Spicy Chickpeas to a serving bowl, then drizzle raita on top to serve

DF GF NF

APPLE CRUNCH SLAW & FENNEL DRESSING

SERVES 2 AS A SIDE

INGREDIENTS

Slaw

1 cup red cabbage (thinly sliced)

½ cup fennel (thinly sliced)

1 cup carrot (peeled & grated)

2 stems spring onion (thinly sliced)

½ green apple (thinly sliced)

Fennel Dressing

1 tbsp whole fennel seeds

2 tsp red wine vinegar

2 tbsp lemon juice

¼ cup olive oil

1 tsp coconut sugar

¼ tsp pink salt

METHOD

1. Heat fennel seeds in a small fry pan on medium-high heat until fragrant. Remove from the heat and grind in a mortar and pestle until fine. Transfer ground seeds to a small bowl

2. Add all fennel dressing ingredients to the fennel seed bowl and mix well to combine

3. Add all prepared slaw ingredients to a serving bowl and pour fennel dressing on top. Toss well to ensure all slaw components are covered in the dressing

DF GF M-PALEO NF V VG

JAPANESE TOFU BOWL

SERVES 2

INGREDIENTS

100g (3.5oz) gluten free buckwheat soba noodles

4 tbsp Zing'n Tamari Dressing

1 cup firm tofu (rinsed and cut into cubes)

avocado oil

¼ cup spring onion (finely sliced)

see page 230

¼ cup carrot (peeled into long strips)

¼ cup red radish (thinly sliced)

bird's eye chilli (thinly sliced)

2 tbsp fried shallots

4 sprigs fresh coriander

1 lime (cut in quarters)

METHOD

1. Cook soba noodles as per packet instructions. Once cooked, drain liquid and place in a medium bowl with 2 tbsp of Zing'n Tamari Dressing and toss until combined

2. Place the tofu in a small bowl and add the remaining 2 tbsp of Zing'n Tamari Dressing

3. Lightly grease a small fry pan with avocado oil and place on medium heat

4. Add tofu cubes and cook for 1-2 minutes then flip and repeat on the other side. Cooking time will depend on how crispy you like your tofu. Remove from the pan and set aside

5. Divide noodles into 2 bowls

6. Add toppings by dividing shallots, carrot, radish and tofu between the 2 bowls

7. Top with sliced chilli, fried shallots, fresh coriander and a wedge of lime

DF GF NF V VG

92

STICKY CHICKPEA & APPLE BOWL

SERVES 1

INGREDIENTS

1-2 tsp olive oil

½ cup canned chickpeas (rinsed & drained)

1 tsp cinnamon

pinch of salt

¼ cup raw cashews

1 tbsp pure maple syrup

2 cups kale (washed & roughly chopped)

½ green apple (thinly sliced)

½ carrot (grated & thinly sliced)

2 tsp apple cider vinegar

METHOD

1. Heat 1 tsp of olive oil in a small saucepan over medium heat. Add chickpeas, cinnamon and a crack of salt and fry. Stir regularly for 2-3 minutes or until chickpeas are lightly golden. Add cashews and maple syrup and toss for a further 2 minutes or until cashews have slightly warmed (if your maple syrup begins to burn it means your stove heat is too high)

2. Add chopped kale to a serving bowl, drizzle a little olive oil on top and massage together with your hands until kale is tender and evenly coated

3. Place chickpeas, sliced apple, carrot, apple cider vinegar and a crack of salt on top of the kale, toss together and enjoy

DF GF V VG

PEACHY PICNIC SALAD

SERVES 2-4 AS A SIDE

INGREDIENTS

½ red onion (thinly sliced)

1 tbsp red wine vinegar

¼ tsp salt

2 peaches (seeds removed & sliced)

1 cup cherry tomatoes (cut in half)

¼ cup fresh basil leaves

1 tbsp olive oil

⅓ cup soft goat's feta

¼ cup walnuts (roughly chopped/crushed)

1 tbsp balsamic vinegar glaze

METHOD

1. Place onion slices, red wine vinegar and salt together in a small bowl or jar and coat all slices well. Leave to sit for 10 minutes then drain

2. Combine vinegar-soaked onion, peaches, halved cherry tomatoes and basil leaves in a bowl then coat with olive oil and goat's cheese. Toss together gently

3. Transfer to a serving platter/bowl and top with crushed walnuts and a drizzle of balsamic glaze

GF VG

94

FRESHY TOFU GREEK SALAD

SERVES 4 SIDES

see page 230

INGREDIENTS

⅓ cup Vegan Tofu Feta

½ cup red onion (diced)

2 tomatoes (diced)

1 Lebanese cucumber (diced)

½ red capsicum (diced)

¼ cup black olives

1 tbsp olive oil

½ tbsp balsamic vinegar

2 heaped tbsp fresh parsley
(roughly chopped)

2 tbsp fresh mint
(finely chopped)

METHOD

1. Prepare Vegan Tofu Feta

2. Add diced red onion, tomatoes, tofu feta, cucumber, capsicum and olives in a medium-size bowl and toss together

3. Top with olive oil, balsamic vinegar and fresh herbs and mix well together and serve

DF GF NF V VG

GREEN DREAM BOWL

SERVES 2 MAINS OR 4 SIDES

see page 8

INGREDIENTS

⅓ cup uncooked quinoa

½ Lebanese cucumber (peeled or thinly sliced into strips)

1½ cups sweet potato cubes (cooked)

2 tbsp pumpkin seeds

2 tbsp sunflower seeds

see page 7

2 cups kale (washed & finely chopped)

olive oil

1 tbsp lime juice

salt

pepper

Green Dream Dressing

1 avocado

½ cup fresh parsley

½ cup fresh basil

1 garlic clove

3 tbsp nut milk (we use almond)

¼ cup flaxseed oil

2 tbsp lime juice

1 tsp salt

METHOD

1. Preheat oven to 180°C (355°F) and line a tray with baking paper

2. Combine pumpkin seeds and sunflower seeds in a small bowl then toss together with a crack of salt

3. Scatter the seeds over your baking tray and once the oven has preheated, bake in the oven for 15 minutes or until seeds are a light brown colour

4. Remove from the oven then allow to cool and get crispy

5. Prepare sweet potato cubes and cook quinoa as per packet instructions

6. Combine all green dream dressing ingredients together in a food processor or blender and blitz together until smooth and creamy

7. Place finely chopped kale into a large bowl and drizzle a little olive oil, 1 tbsp of lime and a small crack of pepper over top. Massage together well using your hands until kale is tender

8. Assemble all ingredients into two bowls, drizzling green dream dressing over the fresh ingredients and topping with the roasted seed mix

DF GF V VG

SUNEE SUMMER SALAD

SERVES 4

see page 230

INGREDIENTS

4 cups mixed lettuce greens

1 avocado

1 cup cherry tomatoes (cut in half)

1 cucumber (cut into half moons)

200g (7oz) smoked salmon

¼ cup Vegan Tofu Feta

Dressing

2 tbsp fresh lemon juice

1½ tbsp honey

1 tbsp Dijon mustard

2 tbsp olive oil

1 tbsp fresh dill (finely chopped)

salt & pepper

Serving Suggestion

Fresh pomegranate seeds

¼ cup fresh dill (roughly chopped)

METHOD

1. Whisk lemon juice, honey and mustard in a small bowl

2. Slowly drizzle in olive oil, making sure to continuously whisk until the dressing is emulsified

3. Add in dill, salt and pepper. Store in the fridge until ready to use

4. Combine all salad ingredients in a large bowl

5. Drizzle over dressing and crumble extra feta, pomegranate seeds and dill on top

DF GF M-PALEO NF

WILD CHILD QUINOA SALAD

SERVES 2-4 AS A SIDE

INGREDIENTS

Salad

2 tbsp pumpkin seeds

2 tbsp sunflower seeds

2 tbsp pine nuts

¼ cup uncooked quinoa

⅓ cup uncooked wild rice

½ cup green beans,
cut into 4cm (1.5in) pieces

¼ cup green peas

2 stems kale (washed & finely chopped)

1 tbsp lemon juice

2 tbsp dried cranberries

1 tbsp sprouted bean mix
(or canned chickpeas)

Miso Dressing

1 tbsp white miso

1 tbsp honey

1 tbsp water

1 tsp apple cider vinegar

¼ tsp lemon juice

¼ tsp Dijon mustard

METHOD

1. Preheat oven to 150°C (300°F) and line a baking tray with baking paper

2. Spread pumpkin seeds, sunflower seeds and pine nuts onto your prepared tray and bake for 10 minutes

3. Cook quinoa and rice as per packet instructions and set aside to cool

4. Add water to a medium saucepan and bring to a boil. Once boiling, add green beans and peas, allow to boil for 5 minutes. Drain and allow to cool

5. Place kale in your desired serving bowl and massage with 1 tbsp lemon juice until tender

6. Whisk all miso dressing ingredients together in a small bowl

7. Add all salad components to the kale then drizzle miso dressing on top. Toss together and serve!

see page 8

DF GF VG

SPROUTING GRAINS BOWL

SERVES 2

INGREDIENTS

1 sweet potato (scrubbed clean & dried)

olive oil

pink salt

½ cup raw buckwheat groats (rinsed well under running water & drained)

¾ cup room temp water

4-5 tbsp Zing'n Tamari Dressing

→ see page 230

2-4 eggs (depending on if you want 1 or 2 each)

½ cup alfalfa sprouts

½ cup mixed sprouted seeds

1 cup rocket

½ cup shredded beetroot (optional)

METHOD

1. Preheat oven to 200°C (395°F) and line a tray with baking paper

2. Cut sweet potato in half lengthways and stab the skin side of the potato with a fork 3-4 times

3. Generously cover both halves of the sweet potato in olive oil and season with pink salt. Place each half flesh-side down onto the baking tray and bake in the oven for 35 minutes or until skin begins to shrivel and soften

4. Meanwhile, in a small saucepan over medium heat, add rinsed and drained buckwheat groats and water. Stir well and place a lid on top

5. Once the water begins to boil, turn down to low heat and allow it to simmer for 9 minutes before removing the lid and stirring well

6. Assess how much water is left: If there is minimal water, then turn off the heat and place the lid back on, allowing the groats to rest and fully absorb any excess water for 5 minutes. If after the initial 9-minute simmer, your saucepan still has a lot of water, then allow it to simmer with the lid off for a further few more minutes before turning off the heat and allowing the groats to rest for 5 minutes

7. Using a fork, fluff the groats and set them aside for later

8. Prepare Zing'n Tamari Dressing

9. Boil eggs to your liking, we prefer them soft-boiled

10. Assemble your nourish bowls, beginning with buckwheat groats as the base of each bowl. Using a fork, toss 2 tbsp of Zing'n Tamari Dressing into each bowl of groats. Continue assembling all other ingredients into the bowls, finally topping with a sprinkle of salt and a little drizzle of dressing!

see page 12

DF GF NF VG

CHICKEN SATAY NOURISH BOWL

SERVES 2

INGREDIENTS

see page 72

2 Satay Chicken Skewers

100g (3.5oz) gluten free rice noodles (we used black rice noodles)

see page 236

½ cup + 2 tbsp of Chefy Satay Sauce

1 cup sugar snap peas (trimmed & deveined)

½ avocado (cut in half)

4 sprigs fresh coriander

1 cup red cabbage (finely chopped)

2 stems spring onion (roughly chopped)

Serving Suggestion

4 tbsp of crushed peanuts

2 tbsp of sesame seeds

½ a lime (cut into 2 wedges)

½ bird's eye chilli

METHOD

1. Prepare Satay Chicken Skewers

2. Cook noodles as per packet instructions. Drain liquid and place in a medium bowl. Add ½ cup of Chefy Satay Sauce and toss to coat the noodles well

3. Add 2 cups of water to a small saucepan and bring to the boil. Once boiled add your sugar snap peas and reduce to a simmer. Allow peas to cook in the simmering water for 2 minutes then remove from the water

4. Divide noodles evenly between 2 bowls and add even portions of all ingredients on top. Drizzle the remaining satay sauce evenly over chicken skewers and complete with desired toppings in our *serving suggestion*

DF GF

DREAMY BAKED SATAY TOFU

SERVES 3

INGREDIENTS

350g (12.3oz) firm tofu

¼ cup crunchy peanut butter

1 tbsp white miso paste

2 tbsp warm/hot water

2 tbsp rice malt syrup

2 tbsp nut milk

½ tsp Tabasco sauce

2 tsp apple cider vinegar

Serving Suggestion

basmati rice

baked veggies

METHOD

1. Rinse tofu under cold running water and press out excess water with a linen tea towel or paper towel. Once dry, cut tofu into 1.5cm (0.6in) cubes

2. In a small square baking tin – around 20cm x 20cm (8in x 8in) – combine peanut butter, miso paste and warm water. Whisk together with a fork until evenly combined and the miso has completely dissolved

3. Add rice malt syrup, milk, Tabasco sauce and apple cider vinegar and whisk together. Transfer tofu cubes to the satay sauce and gently fold together so all cubes are covered in the mixture

4. Cover and set aside in the fridge for 3 hours (or overnight if possible)

5. Preheat the oven to 175°C (345°F). Remove tofu from the fridge and set aside allowing it to return to room temperature

6. Place tofu in the preheated oven for 15 minutes, removing from the oven around the 8 minute mark to toss the tofu in the satay sauce and scrape down the sides

7. Remove from the oven and serve with basmati rice and baked veggies (we love this with baked zucchini, green beans, broccoli and red capsicum)

however, you can bake this without marinating for 3 hours, the flavour just won't have absorbed into the tofu as much

DF   GF   LOW FODMAP   V   VG

MEDITERRANEAN CHICKEN BAKE

SERVES 4-6

INGREDIENTS

6 skin-on boneless chicken thighs

salt

cracked black pepper

1½ tsp dried oregano

1 tbsp olive oil (+ extra for greasing)

1 tbsp fresh thyme (leaves picked, chopped)

1 tbsp fresh rosemary (finely chopped)

2 garlic cloves (minced)

12 baby potatoes (cut in half)

½ red capsicum (deseeded, cut into wedges)

½ cup Kalamata olives (pitted)

1 lemon (thinly sliced)

METHOD

1. Pat thighs dry with a paper towel and place in a bowl with a generous crack of salt, pepper and dried oregano

2. Preheat oven to 220°C (430°F) and lightly grease a large tray or lasagne dish with olive oil

3. Heat olive oil in a large fry pan over medium-high heat. Once hot, place 3 pieces of the chicken, skin down in the pan and sear until golden brown, around 4 minutes. Flip and sear the other side and place on a plate then set aside. Repeat with remaining chicken

4. Using the remaining hot oil in the pan, remove from the heat and add the thyme, rosemary and garlic cook until fragrant, then set aside

5. Place the chicken in a large baking dish or skillet, then arrange potatoes, capsicum, olives and lemon slices. Finish by pouring over herbed oil

6. Cover the dish or skillet with a lid or foil, and bake until the potatoes are soft and the chicken is cooked through. This should be around 40-50 minutes

7. Change the oven to grill and uncover the dish. Cook for a further 5-10 minutes or until chicken and potatoes are crispy and golden

DF GF NF

MAPLE TOFU LETTUCE CUPS

MAKES 8 CUPS

see page 55

INGREDIENTS

Crispy Tofu

Crispy Maple Tofu Wedges

Noodles

150g (5.3oz) or 2 servings vermicelli rice noodles

juice of 1 large lime

1 tsp coconut sugar

1 tsp sesame oil

1 tsp coconut aminos

Cups

8 iceberg lettuce cups

¼ cup fresh mint leaves (roughly chopped)

1 large carrot (peeled & finely sliced in strips)

1 large cucumber (finely sliced into strips)

½ cup red cabbage (finely sliced)

1 red chilli (finely chopped)

METHOD

1. Prepare Crispy Maple Tofu Wedges

2. Place vermicelli rice noodles in a large bowl and cover with warm water. Leave for 10 minutes then drain and place back in the bowl

3. Combine lime juice, coconut sugar, sesame oil and coconut aminos with the vermicelli noodles. Gently toss together

4. Prepare all other vegetables and assemble lettuce cups with desired quantities, topping with red chilli and an extra squeeze of lime

DF   GF   LOW FODMAP   NF   V   VG

SWEET & SOUR TURKEY BURGERS

SERVES 6

INGREDIENTS

Turkey Patties

500g (1.1lb) lean turkey mince

1 tbsp whole egg mayonnaise

1 garlic clove (minced)

¼ cup (or ⅛ of a whole) red onion (finely diced)

2 bird's eye chillies (finely diced)

1 tbsp fresh parsley (finely chopped)

½ tsp salt

generous crack of pepper

¼ tsp cayenne pepper

¼ tsp ground cumin

¼ tsp chilli powder

¼ cup gluten free bread crumbs

drizzle of olive oil (for pan-frying)

Burgers

6 gluten free burger buns (toasted or grilled)

cos lettuce leaves

tomato (sliced)

1 cucumber (halved & thinly sliced)

¼ red onion (finely sliced)

sweet chilli sauce

whole egg mayonnaise

take the extra time and care to dice these as finely as you can! this will help make your burgers taste smoother and more gourmet!

METHOD

1. Add all turkey patty ingredients (except olive oil) to a large bowl and mash together well with a fork

2. Using your hands, scoop out 6 even portions of the mince mixture to create 6 burger patties. Use your palms to press the mince into patties around 1cm (0.4in) thick

3. Heat a drizzle of olive oil in a large fry pan over medium-high heat and pan-fry burger patties on one side for a few minutes, until golden brown. Flip over and cook the second side until golden brown and the turkey is cooked all the way through

4. Remove from the heat and assemble the rest of your burger with sweet chilli sauce, mayo and salad

you can also cook these on the barbeque for that delicious char-grilled flavour!

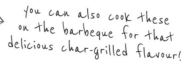

DF GF NF

CARAMELISED SWEET LAMB CHOPS

SERVES 2-3

if your quince paste has been in the fridge you may have to use a fork here to slightly mash it and soften up the jammy paste

INGREDIENTS

1½ tbsp quince paste/jam (or your fave sweet & sour jam)

2 tbsp olive oil, plus extra for frying

6 lamb cutlets or chops

salt & pepper

1 tbsp fresh rosemary (finely chopped)

METHOD

1. Combine quince paste and olive oil in a small bowl and mix together

2. Place lamb chops out onto a work surface and crack a generous serving of salt and pepper onto both sides of the chops, followed by an even dollop of the quince paste mixture onto each chop. Using your fingers, massage the salt, pepper and paste onto each side of the chop

3. Sprinkle fresh rosemary onto each side and use your fingers to gently press the leaves into the paste marinade

4. Allow the chops to completely come to room temperature if they've been removed from the fridge

5. Heat a generous drizzle of olive oil in a large fry pan over high heat

6. Once the oil is hot, add lamb chops and cook on one side for 2 minutes. Flip each chop over and cook for a further 1.5 minutes on the second side

7. Remove from the heat and allow the chops to rest for 5 minutes before serving

8. Serve with your fave salad or roasted veggies! We love serving our chops with sweet potato, asparagus, eggplant and zucchini

this time may be greater depending on how thick your chops are

DF GF LOW FODMAP NF

JACKFRUIT SOFT TACOS

SERVES 4

INGREDIENTS

2 x 400g (14oz) cans jackfruit in water (drained)

3 tbsp olive oil

1 red onion (finely chopped)

4 garlic cloves (minced)

1 tsp ground cumin

1¼ tsp smoked paprika

1 tsp ground coriander

½ tsp ground cinnamon

¼ tsp ground cloves

1 tsp chipotle in adobo

2 tbsp tomato paste

3 tbsp coconut aminos

2 tbsp pure maple syrup

1 tbsp apple cider vinegar

crack of pepper

To Serve

4 tomatoes (diced)

oak lettuce (roughly chopped)

½ red onion (finely diced)

¼ cup fresh coriander

½ avocado (sliced)

lime wedges

gluten free tortilla/soft tacos (heated)

METHOD

1. Place drained jackfruit into a large bowl and gently break apart with your hands. Set aside for later

2. Heat olive oil in a large saucepan over medium-high heat. Add onion and garlic and sauté until soft

3. Add cumin, smoked paprika, ground coriander, cinnamon, and cloves to the saucepan and stir for about 1 minute

4. Add chipotle in adobo and tomato paste and stir well. Once combined, add coconut aminos, maple syrup, apple cider vinegar, pepper and jackfruit. Stir well and simmer uncovered for 15 minutes (stiring regularly)

5. Serve soft tacos warm and assemble with jackfruit and fresh ingredients

DF GF NF V VG

we used a 40cm (16in) wide cast-iron French pan and found this the best pot for the recipe, however, a regular cast-iron pot will work too!

SIMPLE PRAWN & CHORIZO PAELLA

to ensure your rice doesn't stick to the bottom of the pan, make sure your stock is not boiling, only simmering, and you stir thoroughly every 2 minutes!

SERVES 6

INGREDIENTS

olive oil

1 chorizo sausage (around 1½ cups thinly sliced)

1 brown onion (finely diced)

2 garlic cloves (minced)

½ large red capsicum (1 cup diced)

1 cup frozen peas

1 cup cherry tomatoes (halved)

1 lemon (juiced)

1 tsp smoked paprika, plus extra to sprinkle

3 cups chicken stock

2 cups uncooked arborio rice

250g (8.8oz) uncooked prawns (deveined, heads & tails removed)

1 cup sugar snap peas (deveined, tops & tails removed)

METHOD

1. Heat a generous drizzle of olive oil in a large cast-iron pot on high heat and sauté sliced chorizo

2. Once the chorizo is sizzling and begins to curl/slightly char, add diced onion and minced garlic to the pan and sauté until translucent

3. Lower the stovetop heat to medium and add capsicum, frozen peas, cherry tomatoes, 1 tbsp of lemon juice and smoked paprika to the pan. Continue to sauté for 2 minutes

4. Add 2½ cups of chicken stock to the pan and stir well. Carefully pour the uncooked arborio rice into the pan and using a wooden spoon, stir well

5. Allow the stock to come to a boil (stirring regularly) then reduce to a simmer for 15 minutes, stirring thoroughly and regularly

6. While your stock simmers, pat prawns dry with a paper towel and crack a little salt and pepper on top. Press the salt and pepper into the prawns with your hands and set them aside for later

7. Once your stock has been simmering for 15 minutes, add sugar snap peas to the pan and stir together well, allowing them to soften for 2 minutes

8. Add the remaining ½ cup of stock to the pan and stir together well. Lay all uncooked salt and peppered prawns on top of the paella and squeeze 1 tbsp of lemon juice over the pan

9. Cover with a lid and lower heat to the lowest setting and allow prawns to cook and rice to fully absorb the stock for another 15 minutes. Remove the lid after 5 minutes of cooking and stir the prawns through the paella (also scraping down the bottom of the pan if necessary). Do this at the 10-minute mark too

10. After 15 minutes remove the lid and crack a little extra pepper on top, followed by a light sprinkle of smoked paprika

11. Place in the middle of the table, allowing family and friends to serve themselves!

DF GF NF

SORRENTO SEAFOOD SPAGHETTI

SERVES 3-4

INGREDIENTS

Red Sauce

4 tbsp olive oil

½ brown onion (finely chopped)

1 garlic clove (minced)

¼ tsp dried chilli flakes

2 tbsp tomato paste

⅓ cup dry white wine (we used sauvignon blanc)

for a non-alcoholic alternative use seafood stock

1 can (400g/14oz) whole peeled cherry tomatoes

340g (12oz) gluten free spaghetti

8-10 mussels (scrubbed, debearded and checked for no cracks or broken ones. Discard any mussels that appear broken)

8 prawns (shelled to your liking. We keep the heads & tails on)

½ cup hot water

salt & pepper

they should feel bouncy when touched with the tip of the tongs

METHOD

1. Heat 2 tbsp of olive oil in a large saucepan over medium heat. Add onion, and sauté until softened and translucent

2. Add garlic and chilli and continuously stir for 2 minutes before adding tomato paste. Cook until sauce looks like it is almost sticking to the bottom of the pot

3. To deglaze the pan, add white wine and continue to stir for a further 4-5 minutes until you can smell no alcohol

4. Once the alcohol has been cooked out, add the tomatoes and reduce heat to low. Taste for seasoning and add salt and pepper. Keep sauce on low for about 5-10 minutes depending on how thick and reduced you like it. If it reduces too much, add a touch of water

5. Prepare spaghetti as per packet instructions

we use a large cast-iron pot

when you deglaze, you remove the residue from the bottom of the pan and add more flavour to your dish!

6. Add a generous drizzle of remaining olive oil to a separate fry pan and heat on medium-high heat. Place prawns in the pan and cook until the tail turns light pink. Flip over and cook on the other side. Remove from the pan and set aside

1-2 tbsp

7. Place mussels in the same pan, add ½ cup of hot water and immediately cover with a lid (be careful as the water may sizzle). Steam for 4-5 minutes shaking the pan once to distribute the mussels

8. Check the mussels by lifting the lid, all the mussels should be open now but if not, place the lid back on and cook for a further 1-2 minutes. If any have not opened after this time discard them

9. Add spaghetti, mussels and prawns to the sauce fry pan. Give a good stir to combine and make sure all ingredients are evenly coated! Add lemon wedges and garnish with parsley before serving

or until mussels begin to open!

DF GF NF

121

BAKED TUNA MORNAY

SERVES 4

ours is a blend of maize, tapioca and rice

INGREDIENTS

Cheesy Sauce

¼ cup coconut oil + extra for greasing

¼ cup <u>gluten free flour</u>

1 can (400ml/14fl oz) coconut milk (full fat)

1 tsp Dijon mustard

¼ cup nutritional yeast (+ extra topping)

½ tsp garlic powder

salt & pepper

½ cup water

Filling

250g (8.8oz) buckwheat pasta

1 cup broccoli florets

2 medium cans of tuna (around 400g/14oz)

¼ cup spring onion (finely sliced)

¼ cup gluten free bread crumbs
(we used rice crumbs)

1 tsp sweet paprika

salt

METHOD

1. Preheat oven to 180°C (355°F) and grease a ceramic baking dish or lasagne tray with coconut oil

2. In a large pot/saucepan, on medium heat melt coconut oil and whisk in gluten free flour until well combined

3. Pour in the entire can of coconut milk and alternate between whisking thoroughly and stirring with a wooden spoon until the consistency is smooth and thick. This will take a few minutes of whisking/mixing . . . be patient

4. Reduce heat to low and stir in Dijon mustard, nutritional yeast, garlic powder, salt and a crack of black pepper. Stir together with a wooden spoon then add in ½ cup of water (or more) to return to a smooth, creamy, and cheesy sauce-like consistency

5. Remove cheese sauce from the heat. Cook buckwheat pasta in a separate saucepan as per packet instructions

6. Add cooked pasta, broccoli florets, tuna and spring onion into the cheesy sauce and fold until evenly combined

7. Transfer into a large ceramic baking dish or lasagne tray and sprinkle gluten free breadcrumbs, paprika, salt and a little nutritional yeast on top

8. Bake in the oven for 15 minutes or until the top becomes golden and crispy. Enjoy!

DF GF NF

SIMPLE PALEO LAMB SHANKS

SERVES 4

INGREDIENTS

3 tbsp olive oil

cracked salt & pepper

4 small lamb shanks (approximately 800g/1.7lb)

1 small brown onion (diced)

4 garlic cloves (minced)

3 cans cherry tomatoes

2 sprigs fresh rosemary

4 sprigs fresh thyme

3 tbsp white balsamic vinegar

1½ cups water

METHOD

1. Preheat oven to 170°C (340°F)

2. Place lamb shanks out on a work surface and generously coat in cracked salt and a little cracked pepper. Gently press salt and pepper into the meat with your hands

3. Heat olive oil on medium-high heat in a cast-iron pot (or large saucepan). Once the oil is hot, add lamb and cook until browned. Continue to rotate so they are evenly cooked then remove from heat and set aside

4. Reduce to medium heat and add diced onion. Cook until translucent then add garlic and continuously stir for 1 minute

5. Add all ingredients to the pot including the lamb and stir to combine

6. Lightly wet a sheet of baking paper and place it on top of the mixture before placing the lid on the pot. Place in preheated oven for 2 hours and 20 minutes

7. Remove from the oven and serve with a side of baked vegetables

or use in lamb ragù!

DF GF M-PALEO NF

LAMB RAGÙ

SERVES 3-4

INGREDIENTS

1 serving Simple Paleo Lamb Shanks

1 pack (approx 350g/12.3oz) gluten free pappardelle pasta (or pasta of your choice)

lamb shanks take approximately 2 hours to cook

METHOD

1. Prepare Simple Paleo Lamb Shanks

2. When your lamb shanks are almost done prepare pasta as per packet instructions then toss through a drizzle of olive oil to stop the pasta from sticking together

3. Remove lamb shanks from the pot and shred lamb from the bone

4. Add pasta and meat into the pot and toss through the sauce until evenly combined before serving!

DF GF NF

TROPICAL TURMERIC FISH CURRY

SERVES 4

seeds removed and roughly chopped, add another if you like your curry spicy

INGREDIENTS

1 long red chilli

2 stalks of lemongrass (white part only & roughly chopped)

4 garlic cloves (minced)

5cm (2in) piece ginger (peeled & roughly chopped)

1cm (0.4in) piece fresh turmeric (peeled & roughly chopped)

½ medium red onion (roughly chopped)

2 tbsp coconut oil (melted)

400ml (14fl oz) can coconut cream (cream separated from the milk & set aside)

1 tsp ground turmeric

2 cups vegetable stock

¼ cup fish sauce

1 tbsp coconut sugar

20 green beans, ends removed & halved

440g (1lb) ling fish or any other firm white fish (skin & bones removed. Cut into 5cm (2in) pieces)

½ cup cherry tomatoes (cut into halves)

¼ cup Thai basil leaves to serve

vermicelli noodles (cooked as per packet instructions)

1 lime (zested and then cut into wedges for serving)

METHOD

1. In a food processor, add chilli, lemongrass, garlic, ginger, fresh turmeric, onion and coconut oil then pulse until a paste forms

2. In a large saucepan, on medium-high heat, add reserved coconut cream and continue to stir until it splits

3. Add paste and turmeric powder to the saucepan and cook until fragrant, this will take approximately 1 minute. Then add the remainder of the coconut cream, stock, fish sauce, coconut sugar and 1 cup

this should take approximately 5 minutes

of water and bring to a boil. Reduce the heat to a simmer and set a timer for 10 minutes

4. After 10 minutes add the beans and cook for a further minute, then add the fish and cook for 2-3 minutes or until the fish is just cooked

5. Add your halved tomatoes then divide noodles evenly into 4 bowls. Serve the curry and the fish over the noodles. Top with Thai basil leaves and a wedge of lime

DF GF NF

MISS ALFREDO PASTA

SERVES 4-5

INGREDIENTS

2 chicken breasts (boneless & skinless)

salt & pepper

2 tbsp olive oil

3 cups cauliflower florets (steamed until soft)

½ cup nutritional yeast

2 cups chicken stock

½ cup eschalot (finely diced)

1½ tsp garlic (minced)

350g (12.3oz) gluten free fettuccine pasta

3 cups baby spinach

2 tbsp fresh parsley (finely chopped)

METHOD

1. Lay out chicken breast on a work surface and season with ½ tsp of pink salt and a generous crack of pepper on both sides. Use your fingers to gently press the salt and pepper into the chicken

2. Heat 1 tbsp of olive oil in a large fry pan over medium heat. Once the oil is hot, add the chicken to the pan and cook on one side for 4 minutes. Flip both breasts over and cook for a further 4 minutes. Remove chicken from heat and set aside to slightly cool before slicing into thin strips

3. Place steamed cauliflower, nutritional yeast, ½ tsp pink salt, a generous crack of black pepper and 1 cup of chicken stock into a food processor and blitz for a few minutes until smooth and creamy. Be patient here! The key is to get the cauliflower sauce creamy and of the smoothest consistency!

4. Heat remaining olive oil in a large cast-iron pot or saucepan on medium-high heat. Once the oil is heated, add eschalot then minced garlic. Using a wooden spoon, sauté until fragrant and onion is soft and translucent

5. Add your creamy cauliflower sauce to the saucepan and combine with the sautéed eschalot and garlic. Once combined, pour the remainder of your chicken stock into the saucepan and bring the sauce to a simmer

6. While your sauce simmers and slightly reduces, cook the gluten free fettuccine as per packet instructions in a separate saucepan of boiling water (add a little salt to the boiling water)

7. Add baby spinach to the simmering cauliflower sauce and fold through, allowing the baby spinach to wilt

8. Once pasta is cooked al dente, drain from the water and transfer the drained pasta and chicken strips to the cauliflower sauce and fold together

9. Allow all components of the chicken alfredo pasta to thoroughly heat and cook through. Sprinkle a little fresh parsley, a crack of pepper and pink salt on top before serving!

DF GF NF

AVOLUTELY CREAMY CARBONARA

SERVES 3-4

INGREDIENTS

1 tbsp olive oil

5-6 rashers nitrate-free bacon (diced)

4 button mushrooms (thoroughly washed & thinly sliced)

2 garlic cloves (minced)

½ brown onion (finely diced)

1 large ripe avocado

1 large egg

½ lemon (juiced)

2 tbsp almond milk (unsweetened)

2 tbsp fresh parsley

2 tbsp nutritional yeast

salt & pepper

300g (10.5oz) buckwheat pasta (or your fave gluten free pasta)

2 large zucchini (spiralized into zoodles)

see page 7

METHOD

1. Heat olive oil in a large saucepan and sauté bacon, mushrooms, garlic and onion until fragrant and onions are soft. Remove from the heat

2. In a high-speed blender or food processor, blitz avocado, egg, lemon juice, almond milk, parsley, nutritional yeast, salt and pepper until smooth and creamy

3. Boil a large saucepan of water and cook pasta according to packet instructions.

   Add zoodles (spiralized zucchini) for the final 2-5 minutes allowing them to soften and lightly cook

4. Drain pasta and place in the large saucepan (with bacon mix). Over low heat on the stove, gently fold in avocado sauce (add extra salt and pepper to taste) until evenly combined and hot

5. For an extra kick of protein add shredded chicken breast to the pasta!

DF GF

SWEET BUTTERNUT CHEESY PASTA

the key to this recipe is getting a smooth consistency so take your time to blitz it properly!

SERVES 4-5

INGREDIENTS

Cheesy Pumpkin Sauce

½ butternut pumpkin (peeled & cut into wedges)

1 large carrot (peeled & cut into quarters)

½ tbsp olive oil

1 garlic clove

¾ tsp salt

1-2 tsp sweet paprika

generous crack of black pepper

½ cup nutritional yeast

½ cup almond milk (unsweetened)

2 tsp tapioca starch

1 tbsp Dijon mustard

1½ tbsp lemon juice

½ tsp onion powder

Pasta

10 sage leaves (washed, dried, and roughly chopped)

4 cups (around 350g/12.3oz) gluten free penne pasta

2 cups broccoli

350g (12.3oz) firm tofu (rinsed & cut into small cubes)

1 cup hot water (keep the water from the drained pasta)

3 cups baby spinach

2 tbsp pine nuts

METHOD

1. Preheat oven to 180°C (355°F) and grease 2 large trays with olive oil

2. On one tray, place peeled butternut pumpkin wedges and carrot and lightly brush with olive oil. Place 10 sage leaves on the second tray, lightly brush with olive oil then crack a little salt on top. Place both trays in the oven, baking the sage leaves for 10-15 minutes or until crispy
and allowing the pumpkin and carrot to bake for 40 minutes or until completely cooked through

3. Remove pumpkin and carrot from the oven and allow to slightly cool. Add all cheesy pumpkin sauce ingredients to a food processor and blitz for 1-2 minutes until completely smooth and creamy

or high-speed blender if you don't own a food processor

4. Cook pasta as per packet instructions in a large cast-iron pot or saucepan.
For the final 2 minutes of cooking add broccoli florets to the saucepan

5. Once the pasta is cooked al dente, drain pasta and broccoli in a colander, ensuring to save 1 cup of the pasta water for later. Place the drained pasta and broccoli back into the empty saucepan/cast-iron pot on low-medium heat over the stove

6. Add cheesy pumpkin sauce, tofu, hot water (pasta water) and baby spinach to the pasta then gently fold together

7. Allow the cheesy pasta to come to a soft boil and heat well. You want the baby spinach leaves to wilt and the sauce to become thick and creamy

8. Once the pasta and cheesy sauce is hot and baby spinach has wilted, remove from heat and sprinkle sage leaves and pine nuts on top before serving

DF GF V VG

LEMONGRASS & GINGER BABY SNAPPER

SERVES 2

ask your fishmonger to scale, gut and rinse your snapper. you can even let them know you're going to cook it whole so they may offer to trim off the fins and make slits in the flesh for you. If not, just ask!!

INGREDIENTS

whole baby red snapper

1 makrut lime leaf (thinly sliced)

2 cloves of garlic (thinly sliced)

1 lemongrass stalk (white part only & thinly sliced)

4 coriander roots including stems (washed & finely chopped)

2 tbsp ginger (thinly sliced)

2 red bird's eye chillies (coarsely chopped)

3 tbsp olive oil

salt & pepper

lime juice from ½ a lime

Serving Suggestion

½ lime (cut into wedges)

½ bunch fresh coriander (washed)

METHOD

1. In a large bowl add lime leaf, garlic, lemongrass, coriander root, ginger, chilli, olive oil and a pinch of salt and crack of pepper. Combine and set aside

2. Rinse the fish well under cold running water and pat dry with paper towel

3. Using a sharp knife cut two slits not too deep, diagonally across the flesh of the fish

   if the fishmonger cut the slits in the flesh for you, skip this step!

4. Place the fish into the large bowl with the marinade and using your hands coat the fish evenly ensuring to also get inside the cavity of the fish. Cover the bowl and set aside in the fridge to marinate for 3 hours

   if time permits, for more flavour you can marinate overnight!

5. Once your fish has been marinating for 3+ hours, preheat your oven to 220°C (430°F) and line a baking tray with baking paper

6. Place marinated fish onto your prepared baking tray and pour the remaining marinade evenly over the fish

7. Place in the oven and bake for 18-20 minutes

8. Remove from the oven and give a good squeeze with the lime juice. Serve with lime wedges, fresh coriander and a side salad

   this may differ a little depending on how big your fish is. A good way to check is to take a fork and check that the flesh pulls away easily and flakes!

DF GF M-PALEO NF

CARAMELISED GODDESS PIZZA

MAKES 6 SLICES

see page 80

see page 235

INGREDIENTS

1 large gluten free pizza base (or the GF Base)

2 tbsp tomato paste

3 tbsp Caramelised Onion Jam

4 jarred artichoke hearts (drained & roughly chopped)

3 baby potatoes (thinly sliced)

⅓ cup sundried tomatoes (drained & cut into strips)

small handful baby spinach

3 slices smoked ham (cut into strips)

olive oil

METHOD

1. Preheat the oven to 180°C (355°F), grease a medium-sized baking tray with olive oil and line an additional large baking tray (for your pizza) with foil

2. Place potato slices on the greased tray and drizzle a little extra olive oil on top of the potato slices. Bake for 15-20 minutes or until the edges of the potato are just beginning to turn golden

3. Place GF pizza base on your tray lined with foil, and using the back of a spoon spread tomato paste on the pizza base

4. Layer all pizza toppings onto GF pizza base and top with Caramelised Onion Jam

5. Bake in the oven for 20 minutes or until pizza is cooked to your preference

6. Remove from the oven, cut into 6 pizza slices and enjoy!

DF GF NF

CHICKEN PARMI

SERVES 3

INGREDIENTS

½ cup almond milk

2 tbsp + 1 tsp arrowroot starch

½ cup gluten free flour

⅓ cup gluten free breadcrumbs

¼ cup polenta/cornmeal

¼ cup grated vegan parmesan cheese

1 tsp mixed dried herbs

1 tsp dried parsley flakes

½ tsp salt

2 chicken breasts (fat trimmed & filleted)

avocado oil spray

Sauce

2 tbsp tomato paste

½ cup crushed tinned tomatoes

1 tsp mixed herbs

salt & pepper to taste

METHOD

1. Preheat oven to 205°C (400°F) and grease a wire rack with avocado oil spray. Place the rack on top of a lined baking tray

2. In a small bowl, combine almond milk and 1 tsp of arrowroot starch. Whisk to combine then set aside

3. In a separate small bowl, add gluten free flour and remaining arrowroot starch. Whisk to combine and set aside

4. In a third bowl, combine gluten free breadcrumbs, polenta, vegan parmesan, dried herbs, parsley and salt

5. Place chicken in the flour mixture one by one, coat both sides of each fillet and dust off any excess

6. Dip chicken in almond milk, followed by polenta mixture, making sure to shake off any excess and place on a plate ready to fry

7. Heat a medium fry pan with the avocado oil on medium heat

8. Place 2 pieces of your crumbed chicken in the pan and cook for 3-4 minutes each side or until lightly golden brown. Once cooked, transfer to your prepared wire rack and repeat until all remaining chicken pieces have been cooked

9. Bake for 10 minutes or until chicken is cooked through when tested with a knife

10. Add all sauce ingredients to a bowl and stir together

11. Spread sauce over the top of one side of the chicken and place back in the oven for 2 minutes to heat

12. Optional: Sprinkle extra grated dairy free cheese on top of sauce and place in the oven to melt. Sprinkle with extra pink salt to serve

to test if this is hot enough, take a pinch of your polenta mix and sprinkle into the oil, if it sizzles, it's ready

DF GF

FAMILY CHICKEN PIE

MAKES 1 PIE, SERVES 4

INGREDIENTS

3 tbsp olive oil

700g (1.5lb) chicken thighs (fat trimmed)

1 cup brown onion (finely diced)

2 garlic cloves (minced)

1 cup carrot (finely diced)

½ cup celery (finely diced)

2 tbsp gluten free flour

1 cup dry white wine or water

3 cups chicken stock

½ tbsp Dijon mustard

4 sprigs fresh thyme

1 tbsp arrowroot starch

½ cup frozen peas

2 sheets gluten free puff pastry (ready rolled)

1 egg (whisked)

salt & pepper

METHOD

1. Heat 1 tbsp of olive oil in a large saucepan over high heat. Once hot, place the chicken in a saucepan and brown on both sides. Set aside for later

2. Add remaining olive oil to the saucepan and sauté onion, garlic, carrot and celery for 5 minutes

3. Sift in the gluten free flour and stir for a minute. Add the chicken back into the pan and pour over the wine or water, deglazing the saucepan

4. Add the stock, mustard and thyme to the saucepan. Season and bring to boil, then reduce heat to low and cover. Cook for 35-40 minutes

5. Remove the chicken and shred (with 2 forks or an electric mixer)

6. Combine arrowroot starch and a dash of water to a small bowl and whisk together (this should be a small amount of liquid). Add to the saucepan, stir well

7. Add frozen peas to the saucepan and simmer until the liquid thickens (stirring regularly)

8. Add the chicken back to the saucepan and stir through. Season to taste and leave to cool for 30 minutes

9. Prehest oven to 205°C (400°F)

10. In a pie dish, lay over thawed puff pastry. Make sure you cut to fit the dish with about 2cm (0.8in) overhanging

11. Spoon cooled filling into the dish and lay a second pastry sheet over the top of the chicken pie, and press the edges to seal. Make 3 small cuts in the top to let the steam escape when cooking

12. Brush with egg and bake for 20-25 minutes

13. To serve, season with salt flakes and fresh thyme!

DF GF NF

POPCORN PRAWN BOWL

MAKES 2 LARGE BOWLS

INGREDIENTS

Popcorn Prawns

180g (6.3oz) cooked & peeled cocktail prawns (rinsed)

1 tsp sweet paprika

½ tsp onion powder

¼ tsp garlic powder

¼ tsp cayenne pepper

crack of salt & pepper

coconut oil or olive oil for sautéeing

Noodle Bowl

50g (1.8oz) vermicelli rice noodles (or any thin rice noodles)

½ tsp fish sauce

2 tbsp sweet chilli sauce

1 tbsp lime juice

½ tbsp coconut aminos

6 cups (or 300-400g/11-14oz) iceberg lettuce (washed & shredded)

1 large cucumber (spiralized)

2 carrots (peeled & spiralized)

if they're still wet, gently pat dry with paper towel

METHOD

We like to cut our noodles with scissors so they're not so long

1. Rinse cooked and peeled cocktail prawns and thoroughly pat dry with a paper towel

2. Combine all popcorn prawn spices and salt and pepper in a small bowl and toss together with a spoon. Transfer prawns into the spice bowl and toss well with a spoon to ensure all prawns are evenly coated in the spice mix

3. Place vermicelli noodles in a medium bowl and cover with boiling water. Set aside for later

4. Heat coconut oil (or oil of choice) in a medium-large fry pan on medium-high heat. Once the fry pan is hot, add spiced prawns and toss for a few minutes until prawns are hot and there is no liquid in the pan. We like to remove our prawns from the heat once they begin to slightly char

5. Use a fork to check that your vermicelli noodles are soft and can be loosened up from the bunch (we always taste test a strand to ensure it is soft enough before removing from the hot water). Pour vermicelli noodles into a mesh strainer and allow the hot water to drain out into the sink. Place the strainer with the noodles under the tap and allow cold running water to cover the noodles. Use a fork to toss noodles around allowing them to completely loosen up and cool down under the cold water. Once noodles are cold, allow all of the water to drain out

6. Combine fish sauce, sweet chilli sauce, lime juice and coconut aminos in a large bowl and lightly whisk together with a fork. Once evenly combined, add in drained vermicelli noodles, shredded lettuce, spiralized cucumber and spiralized carrot. Use a fork to gently toss all components together until all vegetables and noodles are evenly coated in the sweet chilli sauce

7. Serve even portions of the noodle salad and popcorn prawns in your desired bowl or take-away containers. Enjoy cold or store in the refrigerator for up to 2 days for meal preps!

DF GF

WIFE ME MEATBALLS

*Serving Suggestion:
4 zucchini (spiralized into zoodles) or
250g/8.8oz gluten free spaghetti*

SERVES 4

if following a modern paleo diet, ensure you opt for paleo breadcrumbs or make your own!

INGREDIENTS

Meatballs

500g (1.1lb) beef mince

1 tbsp olive oil

1 garlic clove (minced)

⅓ cup red onion (finely diced)

1 heaped tbsp fresh basil (finely chopped)

1 tbsp lemon juice

⅓ cup gluten free breadcrumbs

¼ tsp salt

1 tbsp dried oregano

1 egg

Tomato & Basil Sauce

1½ cups cherry tomatoes

1 can (400g/14oz) diced tomatoes

1 tbsp tomato paste

½ cup water

salt & pepper

¼ tsp onion powder

¼ tsp garlic powder

⅛ - ¼ tsp chilli powder
(depending on spice preference)

1 cup fresh basil leaves (roughly chopped)

the most noticeable sign they are done!

METHOD

we find it easiest to scrape up with a spatula and then continuing the rest of the rotating and cooking process with tongs!

1. Add all meatball ingredients (except oil) to a large bowl and combine well, massaging together with your hands

2. Create 18-20 meatballs by rolling a heaped tbsp of mince mixture in the palm of your hands. Set aside on a tray or workspace

3. Heat a generous drizzle of olive oil in a large fry pan over medium heat. Once the oil is hot, add meatballs to the pan one-by-one. Allow them to cook for around 2 minutes on one side, before gently rolling them over to the other side

4. Continue to roll the meatballs around the fry pan, cooking them for around 7 minutes in total

5. Add whole cherry tomatoes to the pan and toss gently with the meatballs

6. In a small bowl add canned diced tomatoes, tomato paste, water, salt, pepper, onion, garlic and chilli powder. Using a fork, mix well until combined

7. Pour the tomato mixture into the fry pan, over the meatballs and cherry tomatoes. Using a wooden spoon, gently toss the meatballs around in the mixture ensuring they have all been covered in the sauce

8. Allow the sauce to get hot and start bubbling, then reduce the heat and bring to a simmer

9. Allow the saucy meatball mix to simmer for around 15-20 minutes, tossing the meatballs around in the sauce regularly

10. After 15 minutes, your meatballs should be fully cooked but you want to check your cherry tomatoes. If the skins of your cherry tomatoes aren't already peeling off, gently press your wooden spoon down onto the cherry tomato. If it bursts easily and is soft and oozy, then it's ready!

11. Gently toss in roughly chopped fresh basil leaves and serve with zucchini noodles or gluten free spaghetti

see page 7

DF GF M-PALEO NF

opt for zoodles if following a modern paleo diet

BEEF & VEGGIE NACHOS

SERVES 6

feel free to use fresh broccoli/cauli rice here! we always have a frozen bag in the freezer!

INGREDIENTS

Beef & Veggie Mixture

1 cup <u>frozen broccoli & cauliflower rice</u>

olive oil

2 garlic cloves (minced)

½ brown onion (finely diced)

500g (1.1lb) grass-fed beef mince

½ - 1 tsp <u>chilli powder</u>

2½ tsp sweet paprika

2 tsp ground cumin

salt & pepper

1¼ cups <u>carrot</u> (finely grated)

1 can (420g/15oz) black beans (rinsed & drained)

1 can (400g/14oz) diced tomatoes

depending on your spice preference!

you can use a food processor if you have the option!

3 tbsp tomato paste

½ cup canned corn kernels (rinsed & drained)

Nachos

400g (14oz) (2 bags) organic corn chips

vegan cheese (optional)

1 tomato (diced)

sprinkle nutritional yeast (around 2 tbsp for topping)

3 sprigs coriander

Guac

1 avocado (mashed)

2 tsp lime juice

METHOD

1. Preheat oven to 180°C (355°F) and set aside a large lasagne tray for later

2. Place frozen broccoli/cauliflower rice in a bowl and cover with hot water to defrost and soften. Once soft, drain and set aside

3. Heat a drizzle of olive oil in a large fry pan over medium-high heat and sauté minced garlic and diced onion until onions become soft

4. Add beef mince, chilli powder, paprika, cumin, salt and pepper to the fry pan. Using a wooden spoon, break up the mince while cooking and mixing in the spices

5. Once the mince is almost cooked through, add the remaining beef and veggie mixture ingredients to the fry pan and stir together well to combine. Lower the heat so the mixture is simmering

6. Place 1½ bags of corn chips on the base of the lasagne tray you set aside earlier. Roughly flatten them out into an even layer then spoon out the entire beef & veggie mixture on top of the chips. Using the remaining ½ bag of corn chips, stick a few of the chips into the beef mixture. Sprinkle vegan cheese on top (optional)

7. Place the nachos tray into preheated oven to bake for around 6 minutes or until cheese has melted and corn chips are crispy. While the nachos are in the oven, combine all guac ingredients in a small bowl and dice a tomato

8. Remove nachos from the oven and top with a sprinkle of nutritional yeast, guac, diced tomato and fresh coriander!

DF GF NF

CHILLI LIME BARRAMUNDI PARCEL

SERVES 1

INGREDIENTS

Barramundi

½ lime (zested)

1 garlic clove (minced)

½ red chilli (finely chopped)

½ fillet (120g/4.2oz) barramundi

Vegetables

2 kipfler potatoes

2 broccolini stalks (stems trimmed)

5 snow peas (deveined & trimmed)

2 asparagus stalks (trimmed)

to serve 2 people simply double this recipe

METHOD

1. Preheat the oven to 200°C (395°F) and place an oversized piece of baking paper in a baking tray

2. Place potatoes in a small saucepan of water and bring to a boil. Boil on high for 8-10 minutes or until a fork can pierce through easily

3. In a small bowl combine lime zest, garlic and chilli

4. Rub lime zest mix over your fillet of barramundi until evenly coated. Place the barramundi fillet in the centre of the baking paper and layer greens and potato on top. Fold the baking paper into the centre over each other and then tuck the sides underneath

5. Place in the oven and bake for 17 minutes. Remove from the oven and serve immediately

DF GF NF

LUXE VEGAN CANNELLONI

SERVES 3-4

INGREDIENTS

Luxe Tomato Sauce

2 tbsp olive oil

2 brown onions (finely diced)

1 garlic clove (minced)

¼ tsp dried chilli flakes

½ tsp dried basil

1 tbsp tomato paste

¾ cup dry white wine
(we used sauvignon blanc)

for a non-alcoholic alternative use vegetable stock

1 can (400g/14oz) peeled cherry tomatoes

salt to taste

1 tsp coconut sugar

Cannelloni

1 tbsp avocado oil

½ brown onion (finely diced)

we recommend using a mandoline if you have the option. it makes the process much easier and ensures your slices are even!

1 garlic clove (minced)

2 handfuls baby spinach

1 tbsp fresh basil (chopped)

3 cups Vegan Ricotta

see page 234

2-3 large zucchinis (thinly sliced)

piping bag (or a zip lock bag with the corner cut out)

we love this option for a DIY piping bag!

METHOD

1. **Luxe Tomato Sauce:** Add olive oil, onion and garlic to a medium saucepan over a medium heat and stir with a wooden spoon until the onion begins to soften and turn translucent. Add chilli flakes and basil to the saucepan and stir for a further minute

2. Add tomato paste to the saucepan and stir for 3-4 minutes or until it almost sticks to the saucepan, then add wine and deglaze the saucepan by stirring constantly for approximately 5 minutes

   adding liquid to a hot pan to help lift off any caramelised components from the bottom and sides of the pot

3. Add canned cherry tomatoes, a crack of salt and coconut sugar. Cook for a further 2 minutes, stirring regularly. Remove from heat and set aside

4. Preheat the oven to 180°C (355°F) and lightly spray a baking dish (we used a lasagne tray) with cooking oil

5. **Cannelloni:** Heat avocado oil in a small saucepan over medium heat, add onion, garlic and stir with a wooden spoon until onion begins to soften and turn translucent

6. Add baby spinach to the saucepan and allow it to wilt (it will turn a darker green and become soft). Add basil and remove from heat

7. Allow the spinach and onion mix to slightly cool, then place into a food processor and pulse 2-3 times

8. In a medium mixing bowl add spinach mix to Vegan Ricotta and fold together until evenly combined. Use a mandoline or sharp knife to slice your zucchini lengthways into thin ribbons

9. Scoop ricotta mix into a piping bag or a zip lock bag with the corner cut out. Pipe a tbsp amount of ricotta/spinach mix onto the end of each slice of zucchini and roll. Place each roll into your prepared baking dish. Repeat this process until all zucchini slices have been used

10. Gently coat zucchini rolls in luxe tomato sauce using a spoon and then place into preheated oven for 35 minutes

11. Remove from oven and serve warm with a side salad

DF   GF   V   VG

BRUSCHETTA-STUFFED CHICKEN THIGH

MAKES 4 THIGHS

INGREDIENTS

2 tbsp fresh rosemary (chopped)

2 tbsp fresh parsley (finely chopped)

2 tbsp fresh coriander (finely chopped)

2 tbsp lemon juice

1 garlic clove (minced)

2 tbsp olive oil

salt & pepper

4 chicken thighs (skinless & boneless)

1 tomato (finely diced)

2 tbsp red onion (finely diced)

kitchen string

METHOD

1. Preheat oven to 175°C (345°F) and line a tray with baking paper

2. Combine herbs, lemon juice, garlic, olive oil and salt in a small mixing bowl. Massage ingredients together with your hands until combined

3. Lay chicken thighs top side down on a work surface

4. Separate the herb mixture into 4 even portions and mound mixture in the centre of the open thigh

5. Mound even amounts of tomato and onion on top of the herbs

6. Fold chicken over herb mixture and tie like a present with kitchen string

7. Repeat until all thighs are tied

8. Take the remnants of the oily herb mixture (or oil on your hand) and use to coat your chicken parcels

9. Crack a small amount of salt and pepper on top of the chicken then bake in the oven for 45 minutes

10. Serve with roasted vegetables or salad

DF GF M-PALEO NF

PISTACHIO-CRUSTED TUNA STEAKS

SERVES 4

INGREDIENTS

1 cup pistachios (shells removed)

2 tbsp lemon zest

1 heaped tbsp fresh parsley (chopped)

salt & pepper

2 eggs

⅓ cup buckwheat flour

4 tuna steaks

Zesty Mayo Dressing

2 tbsp lemon juice

2 tbsp Dijon mustard

2 tbsp mayonnaise (vegan or dairy-free)

1 tsp parsley (finely chopped)

METHOD

1. Preheat oven to 180°C (355°F) and line a baking tray with baking paper

2. In a food processor, blitz pistachios until roughly crushed

3. Add in lemon zest, parsley, salt, a few cracks of pepper and pulse 3–5 times to combine. Pour the pistachio crust mixture into a large shallow bowl or plate

4. In a small bowl beat eggs until light and fluffy

5. Add buckwheat flour to a shallow bowl or plate. With one hand or a fork coat both sides of the tuna steaks in buckwheat flour. With clean hands or a clean fork dip the coated steaks in egg mixture, coating both sides. Finally, press steaks into pistachio mixture on both sides and place onto prepared baking tray

6. Crack a little extra salt over each tuna steak and bake in the oven for 7 minutes on the first side. Flip tuna steaks and bake for a further 6-7 minutes

7. In a small bowl add all dressing ingredients, mix well until combined. Serve with a side salad and wedge of lemon!

around 1/8 of their original size

DF GF M-PALEO

156

SLOW-COOKED PULLED PORK

SERVES 6 AS A SIDE

INGREDIENTS

1.8kg (4lb) pork shoulder (fat removed)

¼ cup water

¾ cup gluten free tomato sauce

3 tbsp tomato paste

1 brown onion (diced)

1 tsp garlic powder

1 tsp sweet paprika

½ tsp ground cumin

½ tsp mustard powder

1 tbsp coconut sugar

¼ cup apple cider vinegar

METHOD

1. Add all ingredients (except pork) to a slow cooker, set to high heat and allow the sauce to heat for around 10 minutes or until it begins to bubble

2. Add trimmed pork and submerge in the sauce

3. Set slow cooker on the lowest setting and allow to cook for 8-9 hours

4. Shred pork using 2 forks and enjoy in a nourish bowl, pork sliders or pulled pork tacos!

DF GF M-PALEO NF

PINEAPPLE PULLED PORK TACOS

SERVES 2

INGREDIENTS

Tacos

see page 65

6 small gluten free tortillas or cauliflower tortillas

3 cups pulled pork

½ avocado

¼ cup fresh coriander

Pineapple Salsa

2 cups fresh pineapple (finely diced)

½ jalapeño (deseeded & finely diced)

5 cherry tomatoes (cut into quarters)

2 tbsp red onion (finely diced)

1 lime (juiced)

METHOD

1. Prepare pulled pork

2. Heat gluten free tortillas as per packet instructions or prepare cauliflower tortillas

3. In a small bowl add all pineapple salsa ingredients and toss to combine

4. Assemble your tacos by placing pork down the centre of each tortilla and topping with pineapple salsa, slices of avocado and a sprinkle of coriander

DF GF M-PALEO

158

CANGGU PIZZA

MAKES 6 SLICES

see page 80

INGREDIENTS

1 large chicken breast

1 tbsp raw honey

1½ tbsp coconut aminos

1 large gluten free pizza base
(or the GF Base)

drizzle olive oil

crack pink salt

2 large handfuls rocket

1 handful coriander

chilli flakes to serve (to spice preference)

METHOD

1. Preheat oven to 180°C (355°F) and line a small baking tray with baking paper and another large baking tray (that will fit your pizza) with foil

2. Place chicken breast on the small tray with baking paper and bake for 15-20 minutes (don't worry if your chicken is undercooked you will be placing it back in again). Once removed from the oven, cut into thin slices

3. In a small bowl combine honey and coconut aminos to form Canggu sauce

4. Place gluten free pizza base on your foil-lined tray and drizzle a little olive oil on the base along with a crack of pink salt. Dip a pastry brush into your Canggu sauce to lightly cover the pizza base (you won't use all the sauce here)

5. Layer all pizza toppings (including chicken slices) on top of your base (leave a little fresh coriander for garnish) and finish by drizzling the Canggu sauce evenly over your pizza

6. Bake in the oven for 20 minutes or until the edges are golden brown. Garnish with coriander and chilli flakes and cut into 6 slices

for low FODMAP enjoy one slice per serve!

DF GF LOW FODMAP M-PALEO NF

GINGER BEEF STIR-FRY

SERVES 2

INGREDIENTS

Beef

2 tbsp sesame oil (for wok frying)

125g (4.4oz) rump steak (cut into strips)

½ brown onion (finely sliced)

½ green capsicum (thinly sliced)

½ red capsicum (thinly sliced)

½ head broccoli (cut into small florets)

½ stem spring onion (finely sliced)

10 green beans (trimmed)

½ tsp ginger (minced)

1 garlic clove (minced)

salt & pepper

Sauce

1½ tbsp tamari

1 tbsp oyster sauce

1 tbsp rice wine vinegar

1½ tbsp coconut sugar

1 tbsp tapioca flour

¼ cup cold water

*Serve with white rice or rice noodles,
and sliced red chilli if you like.*

METHOD

1. In a small bowl add all sauce ingredients and mix together

2. Heat a drizzle of sesame oil in a large wok or fry pan on medium heat. Once hot, add beef and cook each side for 45 seconds-1 minute. Remove beef from heat and set aside

3. Add onion, capsicum, broccoli and beans to the wok and toss for approximately 2 minutes then add ginger and garlic and fry for 30 seconds before adding the beef and spring onion to the pan. Add a generous crack of salt and pepper and toss together until hot and vegetables are cooked to your liking

4. Remove from heat and pour sauce evenly over the stir-fry and toss well

5. Serve with rice or noodles of your choice!

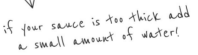

if your sauce is too thick add a small amount of water!

DF   GF   M-PALEO   NF

161

EGGPLANT SHNITTY

SERVES 4

INGREDIENTS

avocado oil spray (or spray oil of your choice)

1 eggplant (cut into 2cm/0.8in round pieces)

1 tbsp sea salt flakes

½ cup almond milk

2 tbsp + 1 tsp arrowroot flour

½ cup gluten free flour

⅓ cup gluten free breadcrumbs

¼ cup polenta or cornmeal

¼ grated vegan parmesan cheese

1 tsp mixed dried herbs

1 tsp dried parsley flakes

½ tsp fine salt

4 tbsp avocado oil

METHOD

1. Preheat the oven to 205°C (400°F), then grease a wire rack with avocado oil spray, and place on top of a lined baking tray

2. Sprinkle both sides of the eggplant pieces with sea salt flakes and place in a large bowl then set aside for 20 minutes

3. Add almond milk and 1 tsp of arrowroot flour in a small bowl and whisk to combine

4. In a separate small bowl, place gluten free flour and remaining arrowroot flour, whisk until well combined then set aside

5. In a third bowl, combine gluten free breadcrumbs, polenta, vegan parmesan, dried herbs, parsley and salt

6. Take the eggplant pieces and lightly pat with a paper towel to remove the excess salt and moisture

7. Place eggplant in the flour mixture one by one, cover evenly, and dust off any excess

8. Place the eggplant in the almond milk mixture and then place in polenta mixture, one by one making sure to shake off any excess. Place the crumbed eggplant on a plate ready to fry

9. Heat a medium fry pan with the avocado oil on medium heat

10. Place 4 crumbed eggplant pieces in the pan at once and fry until lightly browned for approximately 3 minutes on each side then place on the wire rack

11. Repeat with the remaining pieces until they are all on the wire rack

12. Place in your preheated oven to bake for 10 minutes. Sprinkle with extra pink salt to serve and enjoy with your fave sauce!

to test if this is hot enough, take a pinch of your polenta mix and sprinkle it into the oil, if it sizzles it's ready

DF   GF   V   VG

SMOOTHIES & NICE CREAM

REPLENISHER REFRESHER

SERVES 1

DF GF M-PALEO V VG

INGREDIENTS

½ cup frozen pineapple

½ cup frozen strawberries

1 tsp chia seeds

1 tbsp cashew butter (or nut butter of choice)

250ml (8.5fl oz) coconut water

1 heaped tbsp vegan protein powder

handful ice

Suggested Topping

chia seeds

METHOD

1. Combine all ingredients in a blender and blend until smooth and creamy

2. Pour into your favourite jar and top with chia seeds

MONDAY MOCHA SMOOTHIE

INGREDIENTS

1 frozen banana

2 fresh Medjool dates (pitted)

¼ tsp cinnamon

½ tsp vanilla bean paste

1½ tbsp cacao powder

1 tbsp vegan chocolate protein powder

1 tbsp flaxseed meal (or LSA)

1 cup nut milk (we use almond)

1 shot espresso

METHOD

1. Add all ingredients to a blender and blitz until smooth and creamy!

SERVES 1

DF GF V VG

SOUR BURST FRUIT PUNCH

SERVES 1

INGREDIENTS

½ cup frozen raspberries

1 orange (skin removed)

½ large lime (skin removed)

½ cup coconut water

½ cup water

½ cup ice

METHOD

1. Add all ingredients to the blender and blend on low until all ice is broken up and you're left with an icy frappé-like consistency. Serve icy cold!

DF GF M-PALEO V VG

AIRLIE SMOOTHIE

SERVES 1

INGREDIENTS

1 kiwi fruit (skin removed)

½ pear

½ cup frozen mango

1 cup baby spinach

250ml (8.5fl oz) coconut milk (or milk of choice)

1 tsp hemp seeds

1 tbsp fresh mint

METHOD

1. Add all ingredients to a blender and blitz until smooth and creamy. Enjoy immediately!

DF GF M-PALEO V VG

PEACHES 'N' CREAM PROTEIN SMOOTHIES

MAKES 2 SMALL SMOOTHIES

INGREDIENTS

1½ cups frozen peaches

½ cup coconut yoghurt

1 cup coconut milk (or milk of choice)

2 tbsp vegan vanilla protein powder

½ tsp maca powder

1 Medjool date (pitted)

½ tsp cinnamon

METHOD

1. Add all ingredients to a blender and blend until smooth and creamy

2. Top with a wedge of fresh peach and a sprinkle of cinnamon if you're after that insta-worthy smoothie!

DF GF NF V VG

FROZEN SMOOTHIE BITES

INGREDIENTS

SERVES 6

1 cup frozen blueberries and/or strawberries

½ cup vanilla coconut yoghurt

you will have to scrape down the sides a few times and be patient to get a smooth consistency

METHOD

1. Combine frozen blueberries and coconut yoghurt in a blender and blend until smooth and creamy

2. Transfer mixture into a large silicone ice cube tray and freeze for at least 3 hours

3. Repeat the same process with frozen strawberries and coconut yoghurt

4. Transfer mixture into a medium-large silicone ice cube tray (or mini silicone muffin tray) and freeze for at least 3 hours

5. Enjoy as bites or place 3 in a bowl and top with granola and fresh fruit and consume once slightly melted and soft

DF GF LOW FODMAP NF V VG

low FODMAP note: enjoy 1 smoothie bite per serve

COCO-BULLET COFFEE

ensure your coconut milk is inulin free & unsweetened. For m-paleo ensure your milk is unsweetened

VG V NF M-PALEO LOW FODMAP GF DF

INGREDIENTS

SERVES 1

1 espresso shot

½ tbsp pure MCT oil (9g/0.3oz)

½ tbsp coconut butter

1 tsp vanilla extract

sprinkle of cinnamon

½ tsp stevia (or sweetener of choice)

150ml (5.2fl oz) coconut milk (frothed)

METHOD

1. Prepare espresso shot in your coffee machine or as you normally would, then pour into a blender

2. Combine with all other ingredients (except coconut milk) and blend until smooth and evenly combined and pour into your serving glass/mug

3. Froth coconut milk in a milk frother or heat up over the stove. Once warm/frothy, pour into the coffee and enjoy!

GREEN ICY FRAPPÉ

INGREDIENTS

½ Lebanese cucumber

⅓ cup frozen mango

2 cups coconut water

2 frozen bananas

¼ cup frozen pineapple chunks

1 tsp lime juice

1 tbsp fresh mint leaves

1 cup baby spinach

1½ cups ice

METHOD

SERVES 2

1. Add all the ingredients to a blender (leave a little mint out for garnish) and blend for 2 minutes or until combined, thick and smooth

2. Pour into two glasses and top with remaining fresh mint

VG V NF GF DF

ICE CREAM

I scream, you scream, we all scream for

MONKEY NUTS ICE CREAM

SERVES 6

INGREDIENTS

½ cup raw cashews (soaked in water for at least 4 hours)

½ cup raw macadamias (soaked in water for at least 4 hours)

2 ripe bananas

½ cup pure maple syrup

1 tsp pink salt

3 tbsp natural almond butter

1 can (400g/14oz) coconut cream

¼ cup roasted almonds (roughly crushed)

METHOD

1. Drain soaked cashews and macadamias then blitz in a blender or food processor until smooth. You may need to add a few tbsp of water and scrape down the sides a few times to help blend together nicely

2. Add bananas, maple syrup, salt and almond butter and blend until smooth

3. Scoop coconut cream into a large bowl (the cream only, discarding the water from the can) and whisk with an electric mixer for a few minutes. Be patient and whip until the coconut cream is thick and forms peaks

4. Gently fold in the nut/banana mixture into the whipped coconut cream along with crushed roasted almonds

5. Pour ice cream mixture into a silicone loaf pan and allow it to set in the freezer overnight

6. Remove from the freezer and allow to sit at room temp and slightly thaw out (easier for scooping) for 10 minutes (this will also be dependent on how cold your freezer is)

7. Serve with almond butter drizzle, banana and roasted almonds

whisk almond butter & a dash of nut milk together to thin

DF   GF   M-PALEO   V   VG

WATERMELON SORBET

MAKES 1 TUB

INGREDIENTS

3 cups frozen watermelon chunks

5 sprigs fresh mint (finely chopped)

1 Medjool date (pitted)

1 tsp pure maple syrup

½ tbsp lime juice

1-2 tbsp of water (or more)

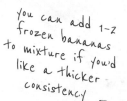

You can add 1-2 frozen bananas to mixture if you'd like a thicker consistency

METHOD

1. Add all ingredients to a blender and blend until a thick, smooth consistency

2. Pour ice cream mixture into a silicone loaf pan and allow it to set in the freezer overnight. Remove from the freezer for 5-10 minutes before serving!

VG V NF M-PALEO GF DF

CHOC MATCHA MINT NICE CREAM

SERVES 2-4

INGREDIENTS

3-4 frozen bananas

2 tsp matcha powder

handful fresh mint leaves

1 tsp natural peppermint extract

⅓ cup vegan dark chocolate (crushed or roughly chopped)

1 tbsp maple syrup

METHOD

1. Add all ingredients except vegan chocolate to a high-speed blender and blitz for 1-2 minutes or until completely smooth

2. Add vegan chocolate (leave 2 tsp aside for topping) to the blender and blend for a few seconds

3. Pour nice cream into a freezer-safe container and top with remaining chocolate and freeze overnight. Allow to stand on the benchtop for 5-10 minutes before serving or enjoy straight from the blender as a thick smoothie bowl!

VG V NF GF DF

CHOCACAO POPS

MAKES 10 POPS → *depending on the size of your moulds*

INGREDIENTS

1 ripe avocado

⅓ cup + 1 tbsp raw honey

2 tbsp raw cacao powder

½ cup coconut milk (or nut milk of your choice)

¼ cup desiccated coconut

METHOD

1. Add avocado, honey, cacao powder and coconut milk to a blender or food processor and blitz/blend until <u>very smooth</u>

   scrape down the sides in between blitzing to ensure you achieve a smooth consistency

2. Add desiccated coconut and gently blitz or fold in until evenly combined

3. Evenly distribute portions of the mixture among your mini popsicle moulds, add a paddle pop stick to each and freeze overnight

recipe only nut-free if using coconut milk

DF NF V VG

OATY CARAMEL POPS

MAKES 6-8 POPS → *depending on the size of your moulds*

INGREDIENTS

¼ cup oats

1 cup water

¼ tsp vanilla bean paste

1 banana

¼ cup coconut oil (melted)

2 tbsp pure maple syrup

4 Medjool dates (pitted)

crack of salt

METHOD

1. Add oats and water to a blender and blend for 35 seconds

2. Place a nut milk bag (or cheese cloth) over a medium-sized bowl, and pour the oaty milk into the bag allowing the liquid to drain into the bowl. Gently wring out the nut milk bag and discard the sediment within the bag (you will only need the milk)

3. Rinse out your blender then add the oaty milk and all other ingredients. Blend until smooth (a few chunks of dates is ok and actually adds a great texture)

4. Evenly distribute portions of the mixture to your popsicle moulds, add a paddle pop stick to each and freeze overnight

DF NF V VG

174

NUTTY FUDGE BITES

MAKES 15-20 MINI BITES

see page 8

INGREDIENTS

2 tbsp coconut oil (soft at room temp)

2 tbsp tahini

1 tbsp almond butter

1 tsp vanilla bean paste

¼ tsp pink salt

2½ tbsp raw honey

METHOD

1. Using the double boiler method combine all ingredients together and allow all ingredients to melt together. To avoid burning, remove from the heat when the mixture is almost completely melted. Mix together well

2. Line a small square tin or container –around 7 x 7cm (2.7in x 2.7in) – with baking paper

3. Transfer mixture into the container and allow to set in the freezer for at least 2 hours or overnight

4. Cut into small, bite-sized squares and enjoy! Keep stored in the freezer

for low FODMAP enjoy 1 per serve!

DF GF LOW FODMAP M-PALEO VG

STRAWBERRY JAM GUMNUTS

MAKES 11 COOKIES

INGREDIENTS

1 cup blanched almond meal

¼ cup flaxseeds

¼ cup desiccated coconut

½ tsp baking powder

¼ tsp sea salt

1 tbsp gluten free flour

¼ tsp ground ginger

3 tbsp pure maple syrup

1 tbsp avocado oil (or oil of choice)

¼ cup natural strawberry jam

METHOD

1. Preheat oven to 175°C (345°F) and line a tray with baking paper

2. In a large bowl, combine blanched almond meal, flaxseeds, desiccated coconut, baking powder, salt, gluten free flour and ginger powder. Using a rubber spatula mix together well

3. Make a well in the centre and pour in maple syrup and oil. Fold together until the mixture has formed a sticky dough

4. Use your hands to roll the mixture into 11 even balls. Place the dough balls onto the prepared tray then lightly press down on each with your thumb so it leaves a small dent in the centre of the cookies (for you to pour the jam into)

5. Use a teaspoon to place a dollop of strawberry jam in the centre of each cookie (around 1 tsp) then place in the oven for 15 minutes or until the surface of your cookies turns golden

DF GF V VG

CHOC CHIP & PB BLONDIE BAKE

SERVES 9

INGREDIENTS

1 can (425g/15oz) chickpeas (rinsed & drained)

1 banana (mashed)

⅓ cup crunchy peanut butter

¼ cup pure maple syrup

2 tbsp coconut sugar

generous sprinkle of cinnamon

1 tsp vanilla bean paste

generous crack of sea salt

½ tsp baking powder

¼ tsp bicarb soda

½ cup vegan choc chips

METHOD

1. Preheat the oven to 175°C (345°F) and line a square brownie tin with baking paper

2. Combine all ingredients (except choc chips) in a food processor and blitz until smooth

3. Fold in choc chips and transfer the batter to your prepared baking tin

4. Cover the tin with aluminium foil and bake for 20 minutes. Then, remove foil and place back in the oven and bake for a further 10-15 minutes or until cooked through and golden brown

5. Slice into 9 large blondie squares and <u>enjoy</u> hot with vegan vanilla ice cream

these are deliciously soft and melt in your mouth. we recommend serving and enjoying immediately, however, if you wish to store them, consume within 2 days and store in the fridge as they're super moist!

for low FODMAP enjoy 1 blondie per serve!

DF   GF   LOW FODMAP   V   VG

ALMOND CINNAMON SCROLLS

MAKES 8-10 SCROLLS

INGREDIENTS

Dough

2 cups blanched almond meal

¾ cup tapioca starch

1 tsp baking powder

½ tsp pink salt

1 tsp cinnamon

2 large eggs

2 tbsp pure maple syrup

2 tsp vanilla bean paste

⅓ cup coconut oil (melted)

¼ cup gluten free flour + more for rolling

1 tbsp coconut sugar

ours is a mix of maize, tapioca and rice!

Filling

2 tbsp pure maple syrup

1 tsp vanilla bean paste

1½ tbsp cinnamon

1 tbsp coconut sugar

Glaze

½ cup canned coconut milk

2 tbsp pure maple syrup

1 tbsp vanilla bean paste

sprinkle cinnamon

only glaze scrolls that you are going to eat immediately!

METHOD

1. Preheat oven to 180°C (355°F) and prepare a large tray with baking paper along with another A4 sized sheet of baking paper and set aside for later

2. **Glaze:** In a small saucepan over low-medium heat, add all glaze ingredients (except cinnamon) and whisk until you've created a gooey mixture (approximately 4 minutes) then set aside in the fridge to thicken

3. **Dough:** Combine blanched almond meal, tapioca starch, baking powder, salt and cinnamon in a large bowl and mix together

4. In a separate bowl, whisk together eggs, 2 tbsp maple syrup, 2 tsp vanilla and melted coconut oil then add to the dry ingredients bowl. Fold together to form a dough-like consistency

5. Sift gluten free flour over batter and fold together with a cake spatula until combined

6. Place a sheet of baking paper down on your bench, approx. 30cm (12in), and sift 2 tbsp gluten free flour over the length of the baking paper then flatten the batter evenly onto the baking sheet using your rubber spatula. Keep it approximately 1cm (0.4in) thick. We used the sides of the spatula to cut the edges and make it square (add the offcuts to shorter areas)

7. Combine all filling ingredients in a small bowl then spread the mixture over your dough with a pastry brush and sprinkle coconut sugar on top

8. Use the baking paper (that the dough is laying on) to help roll the dough into a long log and cut into 8-10 even pieces

9. Place scroll pieces onto your prepared baking tray and slightly press them down if you want them a little wider and flat (this helps them stay intact). Bake for 10 minutes or until golden brown

10. Drizzle prepared glaze over your scrolls along with a sprinkle of cinnamon and serve warm!

DF GF VG

CHOCOLATE FIELDS ZUCCHINI SLICE

SERVES 9

INGREDIENTS

2 tbsp chia seeds

½ cup almond milk

½ cup pure maple syrup

⅓ cup almond butter

¼ tsp vanilla bean paste

⅓ cup cacao powder

¾ tsp baking powder

1 tbsp tapioca flour

½ cup buckwheat flour

2 medium zucchinis (grated) (roughly 2¼ packed cups)

¼ tsp salt

⅓ cup walnuts (roughly broken up/crushed)

½ cup vegan milk choc chips

METHOD

1. Preheat oven to 180°C (355°F) and prepare a rectangular baking tray with baking paper

   roughly 28cm x 21cm (11in x 8in)

2. Combine chia seeds and almond milk in a small bowl and whisk together well. Set aside and allow the chia seeds to soak up the liquid and become gelatinous

3. In a large bowl, whisk together soaked chia seeds, any remaining almond milk from the chia seeds, maple syrup, almond butter and vanilla

   once they have absorbed most of the almond milk

4. Sift cacao powder, baking powder, tapioca flour and buckwheat flour into the almond butter mixture and fold together well until evenly combined

5. Add grated zucchini, salt, crushed walnuts and vegan milk choc chips to the bowl. Using a rubber spatula fold together well

6. Transfer the batter to your prepared baking tray and place in the oven to bake for 40 minutes or until the top of the slice is firm and when a skewer is inserted into the slice, it comes out clean

7. Remove from the oven and allow to cool before slicing into 9 even squares. Store in an airtight container in the fridge!

for low FODMAP enjoy 1 per serve!

DF   GF   LOW FODMAP   V   VG

LOVELY LEMON BARS

MAKES 8-10 BARS

INGREDIENTS

1 cup raw cashews (soaked in boiling water for 1 hour)

1 cup coconut cream

2½ tbsp arrowroot starch

½ cup lemon juice

1 tbsp lemon zest (+ extra for topping)

¼ tsp salt

¼ cup pure maple syrup

Crust

1 cup rolled oats

1 cup raw almonds

¼ tsp salt

2 tbsp coconut sugar

1 tbsp pure maple syrup

4 tbsp melted coconut oil

METHOD

1. Preheat the oven to 175°C (345°F) and line a small square (8cm x 8cm/3in x 3in) baking dish with baking paper

2. To make the crust, add oats, almonds, salt and coconut sugar to a food processor and blitz until you have a fine crumb

3. Add maple syrup and coconut oil then blitz until a loose dough is formed

4. Place mixture into prepared pan and press down evenly

5. Bake for 15 minutes then increase the heat to 190°C (375°F) and bake for a further 8 minutes

6. Remove from the oven to cool slightly and reduce oven heat to 175°C (345°F)

7. Drain cashews and add to the food processor along with the coconut cream, arrowroot, lemon juice, lemon zest, salt and pure maple syrup. Mix on high until very creamy and smooth. Taste and add more lemon or maple depending on flavour preference!

8. Pour filling over the pre-baked crust and spread into an even layer. Tap the dish/tin on the counter to remove any air bubbles

9. Bake for 20-23 minutes or until the edges look slightly dry and the centre appears to have a firm 'jiggle'

10. Rest for 10 minutes then transfer to the refrigerator uncovered to cool completely for at least 4 hours before slicing and topping with lemon zest

DF M-PALEO V VG

CHOC PUDDING BITES

MAKES 12 SQUARES

see page 7

INGREDIENTS

½ cup or ½ large baked sweet potato (cooked & mashed)

2 eggs (whisked)

3 tbsp coconut oil (melted)

1 tsp vanilla bean paste

½ cup honey

¼ cup smooth peanut butter

1 block (80g/2.8oz) vegan milk chocolate (finely chopped into small chunks)

2 tbsp coconut sugar

½ cup cacao powder

⅓ cup buckwheat flour

1 tsp baking powder

¼ tsp salt

METHOD

roughly 28cm x 21cm

1. Preheat oven to 175°C (345°F) and line a brownie pan with baking paper

2. Use a fork to mash pre-baked sweet potato flesh into a smooth consistency in a large mixing bowl then add whisked eggs, coconut oil, vanilla paste, honey, peanut butter, vegan chocolate (leave a small handful to scatter on top) and coconut sugar. Use a firm rubber cake spatula and fold together

3. Sift cacao powder, buckwheat flour, baking powder and salt into the mixture and fold together with a spatula

4. Transfer mixture into prepared brownie pan and sprinkle reserved vegan chocolate on top before placing it in the oven to bake for 20-24 minutes

5. Remove fudge from the oven and allow to cool before cutting into 12 even squares. Serve with coconut ice cream!

DF GF VG

HIDDEN VEG MUFFINS

MAKES 23 MINI MUFFINS

INGREDIENTS

2 cups gluten free oats

2 ripe bananas

1 egg

⅔ cup honey

2 tbsp arrowroot flour

1 tsp apple cider vinegar

¼ cup melted coconut oil

2 large carrots (roughly chopped)

1 large zucchini (roughly chopped)

⅔ cup buckwheat flour

METHOD

1. Preheat oven to 180°C (355°F) and prepare muffin trays with 23 paper patties

2. In a food processor, blitz 1 cup of gluten free oats until it becomes <u>a rough oat flour</u>

3. Add bananas, egg, honey, arrowroot flour, apple cider vinegar and melted coconut oil to the food processor and blitz until well combined and bananas have completely blended

4. Turn the food processor on a continuous, low speed and add handfuls of roughly chopped carrot and zucchini at a time, allowing the veggies to blend into the batter. Once all carrot and zucchini has been added to the food processor, blitz on high intermittently until all roughly chopped pieces have been broken down

5. Add buckwheat flour and 1 cup of gluten free oats to the food processor and blitz 3-4 times or just until combined

6. Use a tablespoon to transfer batter to 23 prepared muffin patties and bake in the oven for 25-30 minutes or until the surface of the muffins begin to turn golden

don't worry if it's not super fine like regular flour

DF GF VG

SEA SALT LAMINGTON BITES

MAKES 25 MINI BITES

INGREDIENTS

8 fresh Medjool dates (pitted)

1 cup shredded coconut

½ cup blanched almond meal

¼ cup cacao powder

2 tbsp hemp seeds

¼ tsp sea salt

METHOD

1. Pit dates and soak them in warm/hot water for 10 minutes

2. Drain water from the dates and place in a food processor. Blitz until smooth then add all remaining ingredients

3. Blitz until evenly combined and smooth (a little chunky is fine). If using your pulse setting, pulse 7-10 times

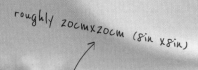

roughly 20cm x 20cm (8in x 8in)

4. Line a square tin with baking paper then transfer the mixture into the tin

5. Use the back of a rubber spatula to spread the mixture out evenly and flatten out the surface

6. Set in the fridge for 3-4 hours before slicing into 25 mini bite-sized portions! Store in the refrigerator in an airtight container

DF GF V VG

LOW-CARB PROTEIN MUFFINS

MAKES 10 MUFFINS

the smaller your muffin patties are the more you will need as this recipe is for 10 muffins

INGREDIENTS

⅔ cups xylitol

⅓ cup coconut oil (room temp)

3 eggs

1 tsp apple cider vinegar

½ cup almond milk

½ tsp vanilla extract

2 cups blanched almond meal

¼ cup cacao powder

⅓ cup choc vegan pea protein

1 tsp baking powder

¼ tsp pink salt

⅓ cup vegan choc chips (+ extra for topping)

the coconut oil will be softened but not melted

METHOD

1. Preheat oven to 180°C (355°F) and prepare a muffin tin with 10 muffin patties

2. Combine xylitol and coconut oil in a large bowl and using an electric mixer, mix until evenly combined then add in eggs and mix for a further 1-2 minutes until combined

   this took around 2-3 minutes

3. Add apple cider vinegar, almond milk and vanilla extract and mix until evenly combined

4. Once all wet ingredients are combined, sift in blanched almond meal, cacao powder, protein powder, baking powder and salt. Fold together gently with a rubber spatula

5. Once there are no pockets of dry ingredients in the mixture, gently fold in vegan choc chips

6. Using a tablespoon, evenly fill each muffin patty and sprinkle a few extra choc chips on top. Place muffins in the preheated oven for 22 minutes or until a skewer can be inserted in the center of a muffin and removed cleanly. Remove from the oven and enjoy warm!

DF GF VG

CHOC BANANA POPSICLES

MAKES 8 POPS

INGREDIENTS

1 cup vegan choc chips

4 ripe bananas

⅓ cup buckwheat groats

⅓ cup crunchy peanut butter

8 popsicle sticks

Toppings of choice

METHOD

see page 8

1. Prepare a baking tray with baking paper
2. Use the double boiler method to melt vegan choc chips then remove from the heat
3. Peel bananas and cut each in half. Slide the base of each banana onto a popsicle stick
4. Pour buckwheat groats onto a plate and have your ⅓ cup of crunchy peanut butter ready
5. Coat each banana pop in a layer of crunchy peanut butter
6. Once your banana is thoroughly covered in the peanut butter, roll it around on the plate of buckwheat groats (or crunchy ingredient of choice)

don't be afraid to use your hands and lightly press the buckwheat groats into the peanut butter so it sticks properly

7. Dip/roll the peanut butter and buckwheat groat-covered banana in the melted chocolate. So the crunchy elements don't fall off, we like to use a spoon or rubber spatula to help drizzle chocolate all over the banana until evenly coated
8. Place coated bananas onto the baking tray and place in the freezer to set for at least 3 hours
9. Remove from the freezer and allow to sit at room temperature for 5-10 minutes before eating!
10. Feel free to play around with this recipe and create your own favourite combinations. We also love sultanas, coconut and maple syrup underneath the chocolate!

make sure to remove chocolate from the heat just before it's completely melted. continue to stir until smooth

DF GF V VG

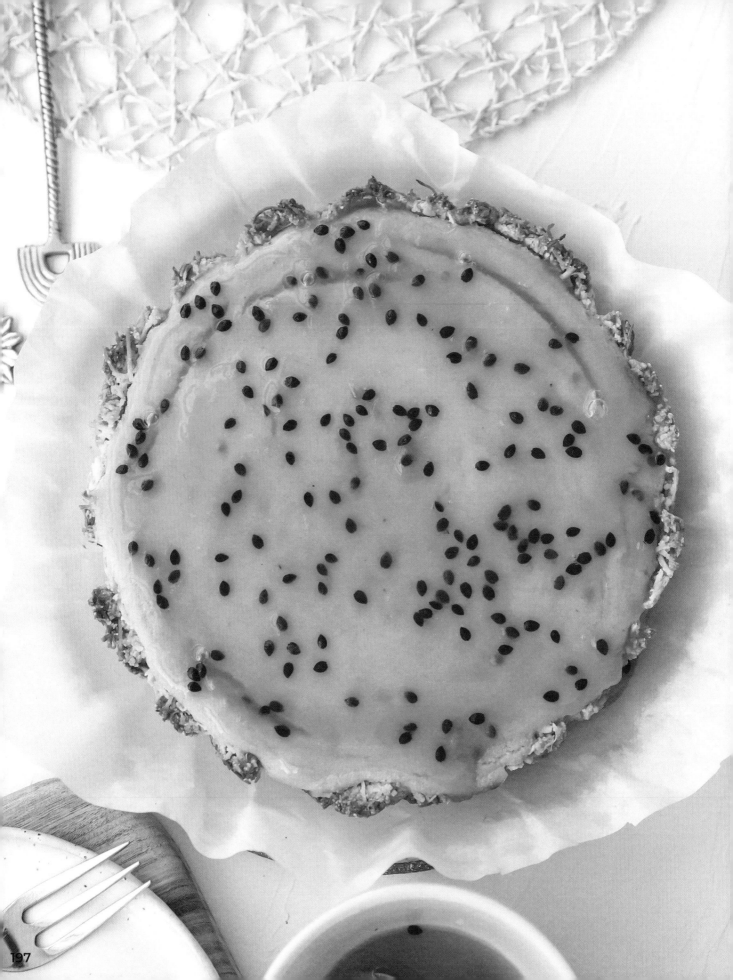

PASSIONFRUIT & LEMON CHEESECAKE

MAKES 12-14 SLICES

if passionfruit is in season, use the pulp from 4 passionfruits. alternatively, you can use 1/2 a can of passionfruit pulp!

INGREDIENTS

Crust

2 cups shredded coconut

1½ cups blanched almond meal

¼ cup pure maple syrup

⅓ cup melted coconut oil

Filling

1½ cups raw cashews (soaked in boiling water for 2 hours)

1¼ cups silken tofu

⅓ cup pure maple syrup

⅓ cup coconut milk (or milk of your choice)

1 tsp vanilla extract

juice & zest of ½ lemon

pinch of pink salt

Topping

passionfruit pulp

METHOD

1. Preheat the oven to 160°C (320°F) and line a pie dish with baking paper

2. Add all crust ingredients to a bowl and combine well. Transfer crust into your prepared pie dish and press evenly into the dish, lining the bottom and the sides of the pie dish

3. Bake the base in your preheated oven for 10 minutes then remove from oven (keep the oven on)

4. Drain liquid from soaked cashews and add all filling ingredients to a high-speed blender or food processor and blitz until smooth (Be patient here! You want this as smooth and creamy as possible!)

5. Pour filling mixture into the base and place in the oven for 50 minutes

6. Remove from oven and allow to completely cool before topping with passionfruit pulp and slicing!

you may need to scrape down the sides of the blender so the filling evenly combines

DF GF V VG

198

CARAMEL CRUNCH PROTEIN BALLS

MAKES 18 BALLS

INGREDIENTS

Caramel Crunch Bubbles

½ cup gluten free rice bubbles/puffs

1 tsp maca powder

¼ tsp pink salt

2½ tsp coconut sugar

1 tbsp coconut oil (melted)

Protein Mix

12 Medjool dates (pitted)

1 cup gluten free oats

2 tbsp coconut oil (melted)

2 tbsp almond butter

¼ cup almond milk

¼ tsp pink salt

½ cup vegan cookie dough protein powder

METHOD

1. Preheat the oven to 185°C (365°F) and line a tray with baking paper

2. Combine rice bubbles, maca powder, pink salt and coconut sugar together in a bowl and fold together well. Once combined, pour in melted coconut oil and mix together well

3. Transfer caramel crunch bubbles onto your prepared baking tray and spread them into an even layer. Bake in the oven for 6 minutes

4. Remove caramel crunch bubbles from the oven and allow them to completely cool before removing them from the baking paper (you may need to crumble them up into separate bubbles with your hands. Sometimes they can stick together due to the coconut sugar)

5. Combine pitted dates and gluten free oats in a food processor and blitz until dates are broken up into small sprinkle-like pieces

6. Add in all remaining ingredients (except caramel crunch bubbles) to the food processor and blitz into a small, dough-like mixture

7. Transfer protein ball mixture to a large bowl and pour the caramel crunch bubbles on top. Gently fold the bubbles into the mixture until evenly distributed

8. Use your hands to roll the mixture into 18 (less or more depending on how big you like yours) protein balls. Place the balls into an airtight glass container and allow them to set in the fridge for 3 hours

9. Enjoy as the perfect afternoon snack! (Keep them stored in an airtight jar or container in the fridge.)

DF GF V VG

CRUNCHY CINNAMON APPLE CRUMBLE

SERVES 5-6

we used granny smith apples!

INGREDIENTS

Filling

3 large <u>green apples</u>
(diced into 1cm /0.4in cubes)

1½ tbsp tapioca starch

½ tsp cinnamon

¼ tsp nutmeg

1 tbsp pure maple syrup

¾ tbsp lemon juice

Topping

1 cup gluten free oats

⅓ cup <u>blanched almond meal</u>

2 tbsp buckwheat groats (optional but adds an incredible crunch)

¼ cup pecans (roughly chopped)

2 tbsp pure maple syrup (+ extra for topping)

1 tbsp coconut sugar

3 tbsp coconut oil (melted)

METHOD

1. Preheat oven to 180°C (355°F) and set out a rectangle baking tray (roughly 28cm x 21cm / 11in x 8in)

2. Combine all filling ingredients into the tray and toss together with a fork, ensuring all spices and starch are evenly distributed throughout the apple. Roughly flatten out the mixture so the apples are an even layer in the tray

3. Combine oats, blanched almond meal, buckwheat groats and pecans in a large bowl. Toss together with a rubber cake spatula

4. Combine maple syrup, coconut sugar and melted coconut oil in a small bowl and whisk together

5. Pour the syrup and oil mixture over the oats and fold together well until all dry ingredients are covered in maple and coconut oil

6. Sprinkle the maple and oat mixture on top of the apples, ensuring it's an even layer

7. Bake in the oven for 25-30 minutes or until the crust is golden. Remove from the oven and drizzle a small amount (around 2 tbsp) of maple syrup on top of the entire bake

8. Serve warm with vegan vanilla ice cream or coconut yoghurt.

using blanched over regular almond meal gives it a sweeter, cake-like flavour

DF   V   VG

LOVERS CHERRY CHOC DROPS

MAKES 10 DROPS

INGREDIENTS

½ cup frozen pitted cherries (thawed to room temperature)

½ cup shredded coconut

2 tbsp blanched almond meal

2 tbsp dried cherries (or cranberries)

1 tbsp pure maple syrup

160g (5.6oz) or 2 blocks of vegan dark chocolate (melted)

METHOD

1. Place all ingredients except chocolate in a high-speed blender or food processor and blitz until combined

2. Melt vegan chocolate using the double boiler method

3. Using a spoon, drizzle a small amount of melted chocolate in the bottom of a silicone chocolate mould then take a small amount of cherry mix and roll the mix into a ball and slightly flatten between your fingers

4. Place the flattened cherry mix ball on top of the melted chocolate in the mould, then using your spoon, top with another layer of chocolate. Repeat until all 10 drops are made

5. Place in the fridge to set for 3 hours

see page 8

we used small silicone moulds around 1cm (0.4in) deep and 3cm (1in) diameter

for a low FODMAP option stick to 1 drop

DF   GF   LOW FODMAP   V   VG

TIRAMISU JARS

SERVES 4

see page 215

INGREDIENTS

12 Lady Fingers

4 tbsp cold espresso

Cashew Coffee Cream

1½ cups cashews (soaked in boiling water)

½ cup cold espresso

¼ cup pure maple syrup

1 tbsp Tia Maria

2 tsp coconut oil (melted)

Coconut Cream

1 cup canned coconut cream

1 tbsp coconut milk

2 tbsp pure maple syrup

½ tsp vanilla bean extract

⅛ tsp xanthan gum

Topping

grated dark vegan chocolate

METHOD

1. In a small bowl soak cashews in boiling water for 10 minutes or until soft. Drain water from cashews

2. In a food processor add all cashew coffee cream ingredients and blend on high until smooth. You may need to scrape down the sides as required, then set aside

3. To prepare coconut cream, place all ingredients into a medium mixing bowl

4. Using a hand mixer with the whisk attachment, whisk on medium speed until light and fluffy

5. To assemble your tiramisu, press lady fingers down into the base of each jar. Pour 2 tsp of espresso on top of the lady fingers followed by the cashew coffee cream then the coconut cream. Repeat this entire process once more, finishing with the coconut cream on top

6. Repeat this process for all 4 jars and sprinkle grated chocolate on top of each. Refrigerate for 30 minutes prior to serving. Serve and enjoy!

WHITE CHOC CHEESECAKE

MAKES 12-14 SLICES

INGREDIENTS

Base

10 Medjool dates (pitted & soaked in boiling water for 15 minutes)

¼ cup coconut oil

1 cup desiccated coconut

2 cups salted & roasted cashews

Filling

4 cups raw cashews (soaked in 2 cups boiling water for 1 hour)

¼ cup pure maple syrup

¼ cup coconut oil

½ cup canned coconut cream

2 tbsp lemon juice

1 tsp vanilla bean paste

6 squares vegan white chocolate (grated)

Suggested Topping

lemon zest (finely grated)

grated vegan white chocolate

this is not necessary if your dates are soft and you have a good-quality food processor or blender. otherwise, you will need to soak the dates!

METHOD

1. Line a springform cake tin with baking paper and set aside

2. Add all base ingredients to a food processor and blitz until a rough dough-like consistency has formed

3. Transfer base mixture to your prepared cake tin and press it down using your hands to create an even layer

4. Add all filling ingredients (except vegan white chocolate) to a food processor and blitz until a smooth consistency is achieved

5. Add in grated vegan white chocolate and fold together with a rubber cake spatula. Pour filling mixture on top of the base and using your cake spatula, smooth into an even layer

6. Top the cheescake with a little grated vegan white chocolate and finely grated lemon zest

7. Freeze for 3-4 hours to allow it to fully set then place in the fridge to allow it to slightly soften before serving

8. If consuming straight from a freezer, you will have to allow the cheesecake to sit at room temperature for 30 minutes or so before serving

it shouldn't be too sticky! you will have to scrape down the sides of the blender a few times

freezing the cheesecake speeds up the setting process, however, it will be too hard to consume. we like to set it in the freezer for 3 hours and then place in the fridge to soften for an hour or so before serving!

DF GF V VG

SIMPLE 7 PROTEIN BALLS

MAKES 14 BALLS

INGREDIENTS

15 Medjool dates (pitted)

1 cup gluten free oats

¼ cup cashew butter

¼ cup almond milk

½ cup vegan choc protein powder

2 tbsp cacao nibs

sea salt

METHOD

1. Place Medjool dates and oats into a food processor and pulse 5-6 times or until dates have broken up into tiny chunks

2. Add remaining ingredients to the food processor and pulse until evenly combined. You want this mixture to be sticky enough to hold the ball shape, but dry enough that it doesn't stick to your hands!

3. Use your hands to roll the mixture into 14 compact protein balls

4. Store in an airtight jar in the fridge and enjoy as a healthy, protein-filled snack!

DF V VG

SUNEE CARAMEL SPRINKLES

MAKES 4 (OR 1 MEDIUM JAR)

for a low FODMAP option stick to 1 serve

INGREDIENTS

1 cup buckwheat groats

1 tbsp coconut oil (melted)

1 tbsp rice malt syrup

1 tbsp coconut sugar

METHOD

as best as you can because it's pretty sticky!

so it clumps into balls. be careful because the tray is hot!

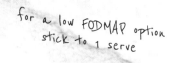

1. Preheat oven to 170°C (340°F) and line a large tray with baking paper

2. Mix all ingredients in a bowl and transfer to the lined baking tray

3. <u>Flatten out</u> mixture with the back of a spoon or spatula and bake in the oven for 12-15 minutes

4. Remove from the oven and carefully <u>break up the flat buckwheat surface</u> with a fork. Allow the sprinkles to fully cool so you're left with clumps of gooey, crunchy caramel goodness! We like to use these for smoothie bowl toppings, on top of coconut yoghurt or simply enjoyed on their own. SO yummy!

DF GF LOW FODMAP NF V VG

SARAH'S CHEWY CHOC CHIP COOKIES

MAKES 11 COOKIES

INGREDIENTS

1 cup blanched almond meal

½ tsp bicarb soda

2 tbsp tapioca starch

¼ cup buckwheat flour (+ extra for rolling)

¼ cup coconut sugar

¼ tsp salt

1 egg

1½ tsp vanilla bean paste

⅓ cup smooth peanut butter

¼ cup pure maple syrup

⅓ cup walnuts

⅓ cup vegan choc chips

METHOD

1. Preheat oven to 175°C (345°F) and line a tray with baking paper

2. In a large bowl combine blanched almond meal, bicarb soda, tapioca starch, buckwheat flour, coconut sugar and salt. Mix well

3. In a separate smaller bowl, combine egg, vanilla extract, peanut butter and maple syrup and whisk together well

4. Pour the wet mixture into the larger bowl and fold together well into the dry ingredients

5. Roughly crush walnuts in a mortar and pestle then add these and your choc chips to the <u>batter.</u> Gently fold together

6. Using an ice cream scooper (or tablespoon), scoop out 11 portions of batter and place them on your prepared tray. Lightly dust your hand with buckwheat flour and gently press down on each ball of batter until it is a 1cm (0.4in) thick cookie

7. Bake in the oven for 10 minutes and enjoy warm or allow to cool and snack on throughout the week!

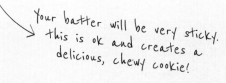

Your batter will be very sticky. this is ok and creates a delicious, chewy cookie!

DF   GF   LOW FODMAP   VG

PEANUT BUTTER PROTEIN BARS

MAKES 8 BARS

INGREDIENTS

12 Medjool dates (pitted)

1½ cups gluten free oats

⅔ cup crunchy peanut butter

½ cup vanilla vegan protein powder

⅓ cup nut milk

2 tbsp pure maple syrup

2 tbsp crushed peanuts

METHOD

roughly 20cm/8in x 20cm/8in

1. In a small bowl, soak pitted dates in boiling water for at least 10 minutes. While you wait, prepare a square baking tin with baking paper

2. Drain water from dates and add the dates and oats to a food processor and blitz until dates have completely broken down and mixture becomes clumpy and sticky

3. Add remaining ingredients (except crushed peanuts) to the food processor and blitz until a smooth paste has formed

4. Transfer the mixture to the prepared baking tin and using a rubber/silicone spatula, press the mixture down to create an even layer, ensuring the mixture is touching all sides of the square baking tin. Sprinkle crushed peanuts on top of the mixture before finalising your compression step

5. To ensure your bars are compact and stay together, place another square of baking paper on top of the mixture and use the palm of your hand to press down firmly over each section. The goal is to make it as compressed and evenly flat as possible! If you have an identically shaped baking tin, you can also use this to place on top of the mixture and press down on the tin to compress the bars

6. Leave the sheet of baking paper on top of the bar mixture and place in the fridge for at least 3-4 hours to set

7. Remove from the fridge and tip the compressed, square mixture out of the tin onto a chopping board. Slice into 8 even protein bars and enjoy! Store the remaining protein bars in the fridge!

DF V VG

PRETTY LADY FINGERS

MAKES 20 FINGERS

INGREDIENTS

½ cup + 1 tbsp coconut sugar

2 egg yolks

3 egg whites

¼ tsp xanthan gum

1 tbsp tapioca flour

1 cup + 1 tbsp gluten free flour

1 tsp baking powder

piping bag

Topping

1 tbsp coconut flour

1 tbsp coconut sugar

METHOD

the mixture will be firm

1. Preheat oven to 180°C (355°F) and line two baking trays with baking paper

2. In a medium mixing bowl add ¼ cup + ½ tbsp of coconut sugar and 2 egg yolks. Using a hand mixer with whisk attachment, whisk until pale in colour and light and fluffy

3. In a separate mixing bowl, add 3 egg whites and ¼ cup + ½ tbsp coconut sugar and whisk using a hand mixer with whisk attachment until stiff peaks form

4. Add egg white mixture to egg yolk mixture and gently fold using a rubber spatula

   be careful not to over fold as it will decrease texture

5. Sift xanthan gum, tapioca flour, gluten free flour and baking powder over your mixture and fold using the rubber spatula

6. Place your piping bag into a jug so that it is supported and scoop batter into the piping bag

7. Pipe batter into a straight line or 'finger' approximately 5cm (2in) long then pipe back over the top to form a second layer. Repeat until there is no batter remaining

8. Place in preheated oven and bake for 10 minutes on 180°C (355°F) then reduce heat to 150°C (350°F) and bake for a further 10 minutes

9. Remove from the oven and allow to cool. Sift toppings over lady fingers. Store in an airtight container or jar!

   you need to work fast to ensure the texture is kept in your batter

DF GF M-PALEO NF VG

SWEET PEAR LOAF ~~~~~~~~~~

MAKES 1 LOAF

1 cup gluten free self-raising flour

⅓ cup almond meal

½ cup coconut sugar

1 tsp bicarb soda

½ tsp ground cinnamon

⅓ cup shredded coconut

½ cup coconut oil

2 tbsp nut milk

1 egg (whisked)

1 tbsp vanilla bean paste

1 tbsp pure maple syrup

1 cup sliced tinned pear

⅓ cup fresh raspberries

1. Preheat oven to 175°C (345°F) and line the base of a loaf tin with baking paper

2. In a large bowl, add gluten free flour, almond meal, coconut sugar, bicarb soda, cinnamon, shredded coconut and whisk to combine. Make a well in the centre and set aside

3. In a small bowl, add coconut oil, nut milk, egg, vanilla and maple syrup then whisk to combine

4. Add the wet ingredients into the well of the dry ingredients and mix together then gently fold in the pear and raspberry

5. Pour the batter into your baking paper lined loaf tin and place in the preheated oven for 55 minutes - 1 hour

6. Test to see if the loaf is done by inserting a skewer into the loaf and removing it with no wet batter on the skewer. Remove and allow to slightly cool before slicing and enjoying warm!

DF GF VG

OAT-MY-GOODNESS COOKIES

MAKES 8 COOKIES

INGREDIENTS

⅓ cup + 1 tbsp vegan butter (We use Nuttelex)

3 tbsp coconut sugar

3 tbsp honey

1 egg

1 tsp vanilla bean paste

1 cup quick oats (roughly blended oats - we used store-bought)

½ cup rolled oats

¾ cup gluten free flour

¼ tsp salt

¼ cup dairy free choc chips

¼ cup sultanas

METHOD

1. Preheat the oven to 175°C (345°F) and line two trays with baking paper

2. In a large mixing bowl, cream together vegan butter, coconut sugar and honey with an electric mixer until smooth

3. Add egg and vanilla bean paste then mix together with the electric mixer

4. Add quick oats, rolled oats, gluten free flour and salt and fold together well until evenly combined and no dry pockets of flour are left

5. Fold in dairy free choc chips and sultanas until evenly distributed

granules of sugar will remain and that's ok!

6. As the mixture is quite wet, use a ¼ cup to scoop out portions of the mixture. Tap the back of the cup gently onto the prepared baking tray. You should end up with ¼ cup portions of the mixture placed on the trays (4 each tray)

7. With a slightly wet hand (this helps the mixture not stick to you), press your palm down on top of each cookie mound until it is in a cookie shape no thicker than 1cm (0.4in)

8. Bake in the oven for 16 minutes or until the edges of the cookies begin to turn golden

9. Allow to cool and serve slightly warm!

DF LOW FODMAP NF VG

for low FODMAP enjoy 1 cookie and choose low FODMAP flour

220

CHOC CHIP COOKIE CAKE

MAKES 12-16 SLICES

INGREDIENTS

⅓ cup <u>coconut oil</u> (room temp)

⅓ cup coconut sugar

⅓ cup pure maple syrup

1 large egg

+ extra for greasing the tin

1 cup + 1 tbsp chickpea flour

½ tsp baking powder

½ tsp salt

¼ cup vegan milk chocolate (chopped into shards)

METHOD

1. Preheat oven to 175°C (345°F) line the base of a springform tin with baking paper and grease the sides with coconut oil

2. In a large bowl, combine coconut oil, coconut sugar and maple syrup. Using an electric mixer, cream together until smooth. Add in the egg and continue to beat until combined and smooth

3. Add chickpea flour, baking powder and salt to the bowl and fold in well with a rubber cake spatula

4. Transfer batter to your prepared cake tin and scatter vegan chocolate shards on top

5. Bake in the oven for <u>20 minutes</u>

6. Allow cookie cake to cool before removing from the springform tin and slicing to serve!

or until you insert a skewer and it comes out clean!

for low FODMAP enjoy 1 slice!

DF GF LOW FODMAP NF VG

To get your base as firm and compact as possible, place another layer of baking paper on top of your pressed dough, then with an identical shaped tin press down on top of the dough firmly, allowing it to spread evenly and level o...

DF GF V VG

NAKED SNICKIE BARS

MAKES 18 BARS

INGREDIENTS

Base

2 cups blanched almond meal

½ tsp salt

1 tbsp almond butter (or peanut butter)

3 tbsp coconut oil

2 tbsp pure maple syrup

½ tsp vanilla bean paste

Caramel

8 Medjool dates (pitted & soaked in hot water for 10 minutes)

3 tbsp peanut butter

1 tbsp water (use the water you've soaked the dates in)

1 tbsp pure maple syrup

½ tsp salt

1 cup roasted mixed nuts (crushed with a mortar & pestle)

50g (1.8oz) dairy-free dark chocolate

we used choc mint and it was incredible!

METHOD

roughly 20cm x 20cm (9in x 9in)

1. Line a square baking tin with baking paper and set aside

2. Combine all base ingredients in a bowl and mix together well until you've formed a dough-like consistency

3. Transfer the dough to your prepared tin and press it down into a firm even layer to form the base, set the tin aside in the freezer

4. Combine all caramel ingredients (except nuts and chocolate) in a food processor and blitz until smooth

5. Remove the tin from the freezer and place the caramel mixture on top of the base. Smooth the caramel out into an even layer using a cake spatula or the back of a spoon

6. Roughly crush your roasted nuts using a mortar and pestle then sprinkle on top of the caramel layer. Set aside in the freezer for 3-4 hours

7. Remove from the freezer and gently pop the entire slab of naked snickies out of the tin. Using a large sharp knife slice the slab into 18 even bars

8. Melt chocolate using the double boiler method and drizzle chocolate over each bar

9. Place bars back in the tin or a glass container and set them aside in the freezer for another hour to allow the chocolate to harden

10. Keep stored in the freezer in a glass container and enjoy these creamy, crunchy, caramel treats!

dip the knife in boiling water between each cut to help it slice easier

see page 8

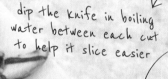

enjoy 1 bar and choose low FODMAP nuts like pecans, brazil nuts, walnuts and macadamias

DF   GF   LOW FODMAP   M·PALEO   V   VG

BAKED APRICOT MUESLI BARS

MAKES 10 BARS

INGREDIENTS

⅓ cup coconut sugar

¼ cup rice malt syrup

¼ cup coconut oil (room temp)

1½ cups rolled oats

¼ cup dried apricots (diced)

⅓ cup desiccated coconut

¼ cup roasted almonds (roughly chopped)

2 tbsp blanched almond meal

crack of salt

METHOD

1. Preheat oven to 175°C (345°F) and line a square tin (roughly 20cm x 20cm/8in x 8in) with baking paper

2. Heat coconut sugar, rice malt syrup and coconut oil in a small saucepan over low heat stirring continuously until melted and smooth (this should only take 2 minutes max)

3. Take off the heat and fold in the remaining ingredients, making sure to mix well so that all oats are covered in the sticky, coconut sugar glaze

4. Transfer mixture into your prepared baking tin, spreading out into an even layer and compressing down as hard as you can with the back of a rubber spatula. The more compressed you get this pre-cooked mixture, the better it will stick together

5. Bake in the oven for 12 minutes or until golden brown

6. Remove from the oven and allow to completely cool before gently flipping out of the tin and slicing into 10 bars

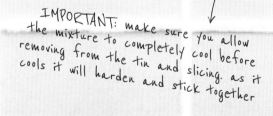

IMPORTANT: make sure you allow the mixture to completely cool before removing from the tin and slicing. as it cools it will harden and stick together

DF V VG

DIPS, SAUCES & CONDIMENTS

COCONUT TZATZIKI

MAKES 1 JAR

INGREDIENTS

½ cup cucumber (grated)

¼ tsp lemon zest

½ tsp garlic (minced)

2½ tsp dill (finely chopped)

1½ cups coconut yoghurt (unsweetened)

2 tsp fresh lemon juice

pinch of pink salt

METHOD

1. Place grated cucumber in a milk bag or linen tea towel and wring out any excess water before measuring to ensure you have the full ½ cup of cucumber then place in a medium-sized bowl

2. Add all other remaining ingredients to the bowl and <u>stir well</u> to combine

3. Serve immediately with celery sticks, carrot sticks or our <u>Prosciutto-wrapped meatball</u>s. Alternatively, you can store it in the refrigerator in an airtight jar!

taste test and add more lemon juice or salt to your preference!

see page 68

DF GF M-PALEO NF V VG

CHIA CHILLI JAM

MAKES 1 JAR

INGREDIENTS

6 garlic cloves (minced)

4 bird's eye chillies (deseeded & thinly sliced)

1 tbsp ginger (minced)

1 tbsp coconut aminos

2 tsp coconut sugar

1 tbsp chia seeds

pinch pink salt

½ cup water

METHOD

1. Add all ingredients to a small saucepan over a medium-high heat

2. Continuously stir jam until a thick and an almost sticky consistency is achieved

3. Perfect on top of nourish bowls, fish, chicken, tofu or even boiled eggs!

DF GF M-PALEO NF V VG

VEGAN TOFU FETA

MAKES 1 JAR

INGREDIENTS

400g (14oz) extra firm tofu

⅓ cup olive oil

3 tbsp lemon juice

¼ tsp salt

1 tbsp olive juice (from the jar)

½ tsp garlic powder

2 tbsp fresh oregano (finely chopped)

¼ cup apple cider vinegar

1 tbsp water

3 tbsp nutritional yeast

heavy enough to add pressure to the tofu, but not so heavy that it squishes/flattens it!

METHOD

1. Rinse tofu under cold running water then place it on top of a clean tea towel. Fold edges up to cover the entire block of tofu then wrap the entire thing in another towel and place <u>something heavy</u> on top. Leave for up to 3 hours to ensure all liquid is drained

2. Dice tofu into small bite-sized feta-like pieces and place into a large glass jar. Add in all other ingredients, place the lid on and shake well!

3. Allow it to sit in the jar to marinate and absorb flavour for at least 24 hours. Store in the fridge and use like regular feta in salads!

DF GF NF V VG

ZING'N TAMARI DRESSING

MAKES 1 SMALL JAR

INGREDIENTS

1 tsp coconut sugar

⅓ cup tamari

1 tsp sesame oil

⅛ tsp ginger (finely grated)

½ tsp white miso

½ tsp apple cider vinegar

2 tsp coconut aminos

¼ tsp lime juice

METHOD

1. Combine all ingredients in a jar and shake well *see Page 92*

2. Serve with <u>Japanese Tofu Bowl</u>, your favourite nourish bowl or store in an airtight jar in the refrigerator

DF GF NF V VG

enjoy 1 serve for low FODMAP option!

GOLDEN TURMERIC MAYO

SERVES 4 (OR MAKES 1 JAR)

INGREDIENTS

2 egg yolks

1 tsp Dijon mustard

1 tbsp lemon juice

½ tsp turmeric powder

pinch of salt

1 tbsp honey

crack of black pepper

1-1½ cups olive oil

we usually add around 1 cup of olive oil over roughly 7 minutes of slow-speed food processing

see page 12

METHOD

1. Separate the eggs as you only need the yolks for this recipe

2. Place all ingredients (except olive oil) in a food processor and blitz on low until well combined

3. Over the course of 6-10 minutes, slowly pour 1-1½ cups of olive oil into the food processor while continuously blitzing on a low speed. If you add the oil too fast, it won't thicken correctly!

4. The more oil you add (over a longer period of time while blitzing) the thicker the consistency your mayo will be

5. Store in an airtight jar in the fridge!

DF   GF   LOW FODMAP   M-PALEO   NF   VG

SESAME & LIME DRESSING

MAKES 1 JAR

INGREDIENTS

1 tbsp olive oil

1 tbsp tahini

1½ tbsp sesame oil

1½ tbsp coconut aminos

½ tbsp apple cider vinegar

1 tsp sesame seeds

1 tsp lime juice

1½ tbsp pure maple syrup

pinch of salt

METHOD

1. Add all ingredients to a small bowl and whisk well or add to a screwtop glass jar and shake well! Enjoy on top of fresh salads or even heat in a simple stir-fry

DF   GF   LOW FODMAP   M-PALEO   NF   V   VG

BAKED CASHEW DIP

SERVES 2-3

INGREDIENTS

3 cups raw cashews (soaked)

4 tbsp nutritional yeast

1 tsp garlic powder

1½ tbsp lemon juice

salt & pepper

1 cup coconut milk

6 sundried tomatoes (sliced into thin strips)

4 basil leaves (roughly chopped)

3 cups baby spinach

METHOD

1. Soak cashews in 2 cups boiling water for 2 hours

2. Preheat oven to 200°C (395°F) and lightly grease a small ceramic baking dish

3. Add cheesy dip ingredients (except spinach) to a high-speed blender and blend for 4-5 minutes or until very smooth

4. Steam baby spinach for one minute and roughly chop

5. Add all ingredients to a large mixing bowl and combine well

6. Pour into prepared ceramic baking dish and cover with foil. Bake for 10 minutes then remove foil and bake for a further 12 minutes

7. Serve warm with gluten free bread or crackers

DF GF M-PALEO V VG

NACHO CHEEZE

MAKES 1 MEDIUM JAR

INGREDIENTS

1 large or 1½ cups diced white Dutch potatoes (peeled & diced)

1 large carrot (peeled & sliced)

1 tsp apple cider vinegar

2 tsp Dijon mustard

2½ tbsp nutritional yeast

1 tbsp tahini

¼ tsp onion powder

1 garlic clove

½ tsp salt

1 tbsp almond milk

METHOD

1. Place diced potato and carrot into a medium-sized saucepan and submerge in water

2. Bring the water to a boil on medium-high heat then reduce to a simmer for around 15 minutes or until the potatoes and carrots are soft and fully cooked

3. Drain the water from your potatoes and carrots and set aside to slightly cool before placing them into the food processor (or a good-quality blender)

4. Add all remaining ingredients to the food processor and blitz for 1-2 minutes until completely creamy and smooth. <u>Serve with Loaded Mexi Sweet Potato Fries</u>

see page 52

DF   GF   V   VG

VEGAN RICOTTA

MAKES 1 LARGE JAR

INGREDIENTS

1 tbsp avocado oil

1 cup onion (finely diced)

1 tbsp + ½ tsp garlic (minced)

2 cups firm tofu (diced)

¼ cup lemon juice

2 tbsp nutritional yeast

1 tbsp white miso paste

pinch of salt

METHOD

don't allow to brown ←

1. Heat avocado oil in a small saucepan over a medium heat

2. Add onion and garlic. Sauté until <u>translucent</u> and remove from heat

3. Add all ingredients to a blender and blend on high until a smooth consistency

4. Store in an airtight jar in the fridge and explore more Sunee Side Up recipes containing Vegan Ricotta

DF   GF   NF   V   VG

NO MOO SOUR CREAM

MAKES 1 MEDIUM JAR

INGREDIENTS

1 cup raw cashews (soaked overnight & drained)

⅓ cup water

1½ tbsp lemon juice

1 tbsp apple cider vinegar

1 tbsp fresh chives (finely blitzed or chopped)

¼ tsp salt (or salt to taste)

METHOD

1. Add all ingredients to a good-quality food processor or blender and blitz on high for a few minutes until all cashew chunks are gone and the consistency is smooth and creamy!

2. Allow sour cream to set in the fridge for at least 3 hours before enjoying on top of our nachos, tacos or nourish bowls!

DF   GF   M-PALEO   V   VG

CARAMELISED ONION JAM

MAKES 1 JAR

INGREDIENTS

2 tbsp olive oil

4 sprigs thyme (stems removed)

2 cups red onion (finely diced)

4 tbsp balsamic vinegar

2 tbsp coconut sugar

METHOD

1. In a small saucepan over medium heat, combine olive oil, thyme and diced onion, leave to caramelise for 20 minutes stirring every few minutes

2. Once onion has caramelised and turned a brown colour, add balsamic vinegar and coconut sugar to the mixture and stir well. Turn heat to low and allow onions to reduce for 5-10 minutes stirring every few minutes

3. Remove from heat once a thick consistency is achieved. Serve hot or store in an airtight jar in the fridge. Use cold in salads, on a pizza or on top of a gluten free sandwich

DF   GF   M-PALEO   NF   V   VG

BASIL PESTO

MAKES 1 JAR

INGREDIENTS

2½ cups fresh basil leaves (washed)

1 cup baby spinach

½ cup pine nuts

½ cup nutritional yeast

2 cloves garlic (minced)

2 tbsp lemon juice

pinch of salt

1½ tbsp olive oil

METHOD

1. Add all ingredients to a food processor and blitz until combined and smooth

2. Serve with your favourite paleo bread, crackers, pasta or as a nourish bowl dressing. Store in an airtight glass jar in the refrigerator!

DF   GF   M-PALEO   V   VG

CHEFY SATAY SAUCE

MAKES 1 SMALL JAR

INGREDIENTS

1 tbsp coconut oil

¼ brown onion (finely diced)

⅛ tsp garlic (minced)

⅛ tsp dried chilli flakes

¼ tsp tamari

½ tsp coconut sugar

¼ tsp lime juice

½ tsp curry powder

½ cup crunchy peanut butter

½ cup hot water

salt

METHOD

1. Melt coconut oil in a small saucepan over low-medium heat

2. Sauté onion and garlic until soft

3. While stirring continuously, add chilli flakes, tamari, coconut sugar, lime juice, curry powder and continue to stir for 30 seconds. Add peanut butter and stir to combine

4. Add tablespoons of hot water at a time (while continuing to stir) until your desired consistency is achieved. Add salt to taste

5. Serve with Chicken Satay Skewers, toss through your favourite raw salad or store in an airtight jar in the refrigerator

see page 72

DF GF V VG

ROASTED PUMPKIN HUMMUS

MAKES 1 SMALL JAR

INGREDIENTS

400g (14oz) canned chickpeas (rinsed & drained)

2 garlic cloves (preferably roasted)

1 cup roasted cooked pumpkin

½ tsp ground cumin

⅛ tsp sweet paprika

1 tsp pure maple syrup

½ tsp lemon juice

½ tbsp tahini

½ tsp coconut oil

¼ tsp pink salt

METHOD

1. Place all ingredients in a food processor and blitz on high until you have a smooth consistency.

DF GF NF V VG

ACKNOWLEDGEMENTS

This cookbook has been more than two years in the making, so I want to thank YOU (my lovely reader) for being patient with me and encouraging me to pursue this dream of finally creating my very own tangible cookbook!

None of this would have been possible without my amazing little sister and incredible graphic designer, Tahlia. You, more than anyone, have been so patient with me as I have created, tweaked, edited, and changed my mind hundreds of times! Thank you for making this experience so enjoyable and not only understanding my vision but truly bringing it to life! This entire book would not have been possible without you.

In times of doubting myself or questioning my process, I can always rely on my incredibly supportive husband, Kurt. You always encourage me to persevere, work hard, and trust my gut. Thank you for being the insane positivity in our household and literally being my hype man. You have taste-tested every single one of these recipes and never shy away from giving me your honest feedback. I love that you now also know how to cook a handful of these recipes (please cook dinner tonight - page 159).

Anita, I couldn't have asked for a better friend to share my kitchen with! Thank you for helping me develop many of these recipes and teaching me countless culinary tips and tricks.

Thank you to my boys, Fox and Malakai. You have been the most joyful taste-testers, egg-crackers, dough-rollers, and dish hands. I will forever strive to replicate Foxy's reaction when he tasted my Naked Snickie bars for the first time . . . "Mum, this is HECTIC!" You take after your father - hype man junior.

I pray this is the first of many cookbooks from me. I have enjoyed this process so much and cannot wait to see you creating these recipes at home!

First published in 2023 by House of Groms
Reprinted 2024

Copyright © 2023 House of Groms

For information about permission to reproduce selections from this book, write to
info@briobooks.com.au

ISBN 9781922598707 (print)

Published in Australia and New Zealand by:

House of Groms
3/2 Clerke Place
Kurnell NSW 2231
Australia
Email: kurt@houseofgroms.com
Web: houseofgroms.com

Produced in partnership with Brio Books

Photography and Illustrations by Sarah Tilse, Kurt Tilse (House of Groms) and Lara De Bruyne

Internal and cover design by Sarah Tilse and Tahlia Stevenson - House of Groms

Printed and bound in China by Asia Pacific Offset